Many peo[illegible] of them believe that wild animals are only to be found living in the country. What they – and you – may not realize is that there are many wild animals of all kinds – mammals, birds, reptiles and insects – that spend their lives within towns and cities. Some commute between town and country. Some spend their days afield and use the town as a dormitory. But there are many creatures that live permanently in the very heart of the city.

From night-time prowlers like foxes and badgers, to rubbish-tip pests like rats and cockroaches and even protected species such as owls and bats, *Town Watch* provides a wealth of information and stories about urban wildlife. So if you live in a town and you're interested in animals, start with your own back garden or local churchyard. Keep this book handy and keep a good look out – you never know what surprising animals you might catch sight of!

Dick King-Smith was a farmer in Gloucestershire for many years and this background has proved invaluable for his amusing animal stories. He also taught in a village primary school but he now writes full time. He has more recently become well-known for his television appearances with his miniature wire-haired dachshund, Dodo, on TV-am's *Rub-a-Dub-Tub* programme.

Other books by Dick King-Smith

ACE
DAGGIE DOGFOOT
DODOS ARE FOREVER
THE FOX BUSTERS
HARRY'S MAD
MAGNUS POWERMOUSE
MARTIN'S MICE
THE MOUSE BUTCHER
NOAH'S BROTHER
PADDY'S POT OF GOLD
THE QUEEN'S NOSE
SADDLEBOTTOM
THE SHEEP-PIG
THE TOBY MAN
TUMBLEWEED
THE WATER HORSE

Non-fiction

COUNTRY WATCH
WATER WATCH
PETS FOR KEEPS

Dick King-Smith

TOWN WATCH

Look out for the wildlife in your town

Illustrated by Catherine Bradbury

PUFFIN BOOKS

PUFFIN BOOKS

Published by the Penguin Group
Penguin Books Ltd, 27 Wrights Lane, London W8 5TZ, England
Penguin Books USA Inc., 375 Hudson Street, New York, New York 10014, USA
Penguin Books Australia Ltd, Ringwood, Victoria, Australia
Penguin Books Canada Ltd, 10 Alcorn Avenue, Toronto, Ontario, Canada M4V 3B2
Penguin Books (NZ) Ltd, 182–190 Wairau Road, Auckland 10, New Zealand

Penguin Books Ltd, Registered Offices: Harmondsworth, Middlesex, England

First published 1987
3 5 7 9 10 8 6 4 2

Printed in England by Clays Ltd, St Ives plc
Filmset in Linotron Baskerville

CONTENTS

Chapter 1

'TSEE-TSEE!'

Most people, the great majority, live in cities and towns. Comparatively few live in the countryside. True, would you say?

I think so.

Most wild animals, the great majority, live in the countryside. Comparatively few live in the towns. Is that also true?

I don't think it is.

You'll notice that I said 'wild' animals, because of course there are millions of sheep and cattle and pigs and horses and chickens that you would most definitely not expect to see in the shopping precincts, or the housing estates, or marching up the high street. Forget about farm animals. This book is not about them.

It's about the surprisingly large numbers of all kinds of animals – mammals, birds, reptiles and insects – that spend their lives within towns and cities. Some commute between town and country. Some spend their days afield and use the town as a dormitory. But there are a great many creatures that live permanently amongst the brick and concrete of the built-up areas, even in the very heart of the city.

If you live in a town and you're interested in animals, don't think that you have to make an expedition into the country in order to see them. They're all around you. Sometimes they're literally on your doorstep, as anyone knows who has opened the front door to pick up the milk, and found each bottle-cap neatly pierced by a blue tit's beak. 'Tsee-tsee!' the bird cries as it flies off with a cropful of cream. 'Tsee how clever I am!'

The nearest city to my home is Bristol, which for many years now has been a centre for the study of the urban fox. Wonderful films have been made of the day-to-day (or night-to-night) lives of Bristol foxes, and a great deal of information has been gathered. Some of the things that have been noted would sound almost unbelievable had they not

blue tit

been reported by expert watchers. Here's just one story, from a book written by one of those experts, of the antics of a fox in broad daylight.

Every lunchtime a vixen would cross a busy main road to the BBC studios in Bristol. She was bound for the canteen, where the remains of sandwiches and other titbits were disposed of. Fortune favours the brave, they say, and day after day she nipped between the traffic unscathed.

She must have been a lucky fox, because when at

last she was run over, it was by a bicycle, and she survived.

Not all the animal behaviour that you can see in your town will be as strange or dramatic as that, but once you start looking and noticing and observing, you'll be surprised just how many and how interesting are the creatures living within its boundaries.

Chapter 2

A SCREAM IN THE NIGHT

Round about 1960, I remember, a doctor friend of mine was driving to a night call in the small hours. It was in a suburban part of Bristol, and suddenly, to his amazement, he saw a fox. There, in his headlights, was a fox calmly walking along a city street. What an extraordinary thing, we all thought – a fox, of all creatures, in a town, of all places!

What a change there has been this last quarter of a century. Now the urban fox is so common that doctors on night calls would probably be amazed *not* to see foxes in the streets quite regularly.

The fox is nobody's fool, in fact it's as bright as a button, and over the years foxes have come to learn that the town is an excellent place in which to live. It has advantages over their usual countryside habitats in several ways.

To begin with, there are no foxhunters in town, neither horsemen with hounds, nor farmers with guns; and in town there is a huge choice of places to make an earth or a den in which to live and bring up cubs. But above all, there are masses of people, and it is mainly they who provide the fox with an endless supply of food.

A few do so intentionally, regularly feeding the fox who has perhaps made a home under their garden shed or garage, so that they can observe the animal. But a great deal that comes the fox's way is wasted food. Man is both a wasteful and an untidy animal, and nowadays, when he chucks away his Kentucky Fried Chicken box with maybe a few scraps in it, there's likely to be a fox handy who will later eat not only the scraps but the grease-soaked paper and even the box itself.

Hunting people have a special scornful name for town (or 'city', 'urban', 'suburban') foxes. They call them 'dustbin foxes', implying that they are nothing more than half-starved, scavenging vagrants, not to be compared with their robust country cousins. But this is not true. Of course town foxes explore dustbins – the fox is an oppor-

'a great deal that comes the fox's way is wasted food'

tunist, above all – where wasteful man chucks away a lot of good stuff; it's a part of their food supply; but far from being famished, they are generally strong and healthy.

Indeed, if you imagine a country fox in the

depths of a bitter winter when the food it needs to keep itself warm is very limited and beetles are a treat, and then compare its lot with that of the town fox who has plenty of shelter from the cold and just as good pickings as in summer, you can judge who's better off (and the town fox never hears the huntsman's horn).

You can see the advantages of town life from the following table which gives the results of examination of the stomach contents of 571 dead foxes.

Earthworms 12.2%
Pet mammals 2.9%
Wild animals 13.1%
Pet birds 5.8%
Wild birds 14.4%
Insects 9.2%
Fruit and vegetables 7.6%
Scavenged meat, bones and fat 24.1%
Other scavenged food items 10.7%

So you see that, even leaving aside the killing of pets (which country foxes might also do), the town fox, with nearly 35 per cent of his food intake scavenged from the townspeople, scores heavily over his country counterpart.

Some foxes live in towns because the town has, so to speak, enveloped them. A town expands and spreads, and housing estates and roads and shops are built on what was traditional fox territory, and so the descendants of those once rural fox populations simply stay put. Some foxes commute, spending their days outside the town (largely to sleep – the fox is mainly a nocturnal animal), and coming into town at night to forage. A certain number commute in the reverse direction.

But there is a large steady population of foxes that live their entire lives within the city or town limits. Usually, unlike the country fox, each does not range far but keeps to quite a limited territory. These townees make their homes in a great variety of places: under garages or sheds; under the floorboards of unoccupied (and occupied!) houses; amongst piles of tins and other rubbish; amidst heaps of old cars in breakers' yards; and in many other unexpected sites. And of course in every town there are 'oases' of land that suit foxes admirably – parks, churchyards, patches of waste ground, railway embankments, allotments and people's gardens. In some of these places there may be wild rabbits and, of course, many smaller mammals such as rats and mice and voles, and in many gardens there are tame rabbits and guinea-pigs in hutches and, especially, hens in chicken-runs. And if these animals are not securely penned, they make a nice addition to street scraps and the food scavenged from bird-tables and compost heaps, and refuse tips and dustbins. There have been reports of foxes killing cats, though I don't believe them. Foxes are not very big animals, weighing on average between twelve and fifteen pounds, and cats can be pretty tough customers; and when cat fur is found in fox 'scats' or droppings, it has probably been scavenged. But I dare say the occasional kitten disappears if the chance arises.

You will hear people say that the fox kills indiscriminately, for the love of killing, out of bloodlust. And certainly once a fox gets amongst a flock of hens, there will be a massacre. I know, because a fox once killed nearly twenty fat cockerels of mine in a few minutes – in broad daylight, too. But you can't actually blame the fox, you can't say, 'Oh what a cruel animal!' because it kills more than it needs. The fact of the matter is that the creature's response is automatic – as long as anything flutters, so long is the fox programmed to pounce and kill. It's a reflex action, just like your kitten batting at the cotton reel you dangle before it.

Foxes are specially active at dusk and at dawn, though occasionally you will see a town fox in the daytime (like the vixen who visited the BBC). But if you don't see one, you may well hear it at night. In winter, and particularly round about the mating season in the early part of the year, those shrill barks are unmistakable – three or four high-pitched yaps, often followed by a bloodcurdling

the fox's shrill mating barks are unmistakable

scream. People hearing this have rung the police to report a murder. And something else that's unmistakable is the fox's spoor, best seen, of course, in snow. If you find a straight line of neat small footprints (much smaller than those of the average dog), which appear to have been made by a two-footed animal, they are fox tracks. For when walking or trotting (always, that is, except when hurrying), the fox's hind feet fall exactly where its forefeet did.

Cubs are born round about March, usually three to five of them. The vixen has only one litter a year, and as a rule the dog fox does the hunting for his family and brings food to the earth or den, though occasionally one will push off and leave the vixen to do the hunting as well as the nursing. There are occasions when a mother fox is killed (run over, let's say) while the cubs are small. Then they will die. And in fact only about six out of every ten town fox-cubs survive to maturity. Those that die are killed by dogs (and sometimes badgers), by flooding, or by cold.

But the average adult fox's life in town is not all that long; only 6 per cent of town foxes live more than three years. Of the whole fox population of any town, around six out of every ten animals will die each year. Some will die of misadventure, like becoming wedged in fence palings or drowned in swimming pools, but a good half of those that die

dog fox bringing food to the earth

will be killed on the roads. This is the price that the urban fox pays for warm lying, protection from the huntsman and the shooting man, and good feeding. It's no match for the motor car.

Chapter 3

BARS, VELVETS, CHECKERS AND SPADGERS

One bird that has completely adapted to town life is the pigeon. I can hear you saying, 'Oh, but they're tame – you said you were going to stick to wild animals.' And of course they are tame in the sense of being familiar and unfrightened, as anyone knows who has watched a mass of them strutting and gobbling round his feet. Not so long ago I was sitting on a bench in a city square, and one of the thousands of pigeons that lived there came and sat on my head, and cooed. I sat very still and crossed my fingers, hoping that that was all it would do.

But even the friendliest town pigeons are still wild birds, belonging to no one, doing no one's bidding. We call them feral pigeons. 'Feral' means wild, untamed, and indeed the rock doves from which these birds are descended can still be found breeding wild on the coast of western Scotland. Probably the most important ancestors of our town pigeons were rock doves domesticated by the Romans and then brought by them to this country. Like most of the things the Romans did, this was for a good reason. Young rock doves were very good to eat.

For centuries after the Roman occupation, up until a couple of hundred years ago, in fact, every lord of the manor would have his dovecot, a sizeable building in which he fattened dozens, often hundreds, of birds to provide him with fresh meat in winter.

Meat-eating, you see, was a very different business in those days. In spring and summer there was plenty of grass for sheep and cattle to graze on, but there wasn't the machinery or the know-how for preserving large quantities of hay or straw for winter feeding. So, at the end of the grazing season, the bulk of the beasts – breeding stock excepted – were slaughtered. That would have left the well-off folk with the prospect of a meatless winter. Even the rabbits, introduced to this country in the late 1300s and kept in specially made warrens to provide meat, would not have bred in large numbers till the spring. (As for the poor, they never got much meat anyway, only what they could poach.) So, for the lord of the manor, the answer was the dove for a number of reasons.

Firstly, it has a very long breeding season, almost all year long if it is well fed. Secondly, it works hard at this breeding business; while the parent birds are still feeding their one or two babies or 'squabs', as they are called, the hen bird

pigeon feeding young squabs

will have laid another couple of eggs and will sit them as soon as the first squabs are old enough. They feed their young on 'pigeon milk', a lovely gooey mess secreted from the lining of the crop of both hen and cock bird; the babies stick their heads in their parents' mouths and gobble it up and grow fast and fat. And the third bonus that appealed to the lord of the manor was this. The birds flew free, to and from the dovecot, and fed themselves on the

dovecot

corn that the poor old peasants had laboriously planted on their little plots. The doves ate a great deal of it, and there wasn't anything the peasants could do but cuss.

There's a fine Norman dovecot, beautifully preserved, not far from where I live. Its walls are lined, from bottom to top (and they're perhaps forty-feet high) with square nesting-holes. I've counted, and there are almost 900 of these holes, which means that the lord of that manor probably

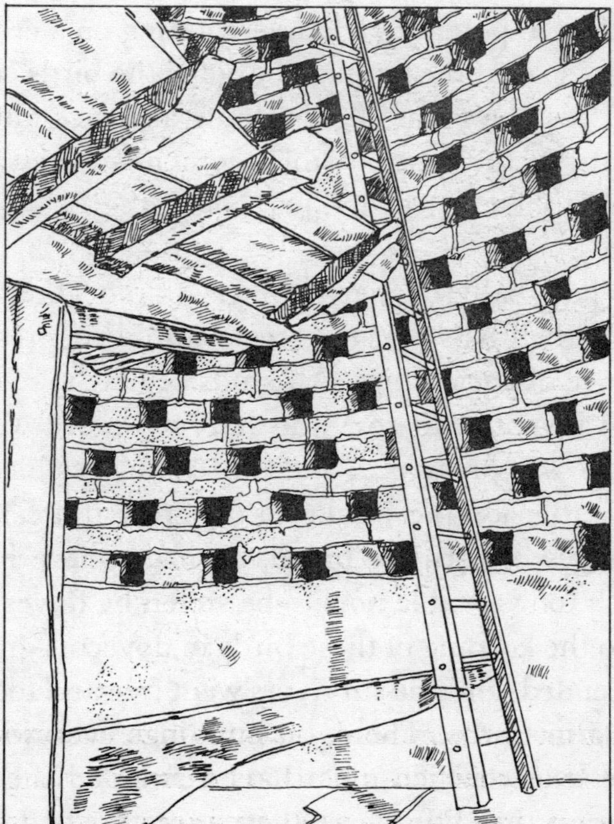

inside of a dovecot

kept between 400 and 500 birds (allowing two nesting-holes per hen so that she could lay her second clutch next door).

At the top of the dovecot is a kind of wooden roof like a miniature house, called a 'lantern', out through which the birds flew to do their foraging. When that dovecot was in use, it would have had inside it a 'potence', a ladder rotating on a central pillar, so that the man in charge of the birds could work his way round the building and pick out the squabs at the best possible moment – when they were at their fattest and just before they were able to fly.

What really changed things, round about the end of the 1700s, was the great improvement in the science of agriculture. All kinds of new machines were invented to sow and harvest, more winter fodder was preserved, and it became possible and profitable for the landlords to grow quite large acreages of corn for bread, corn therefore being much too valuable now to be stolen by doves.

So the keeping of these birds in dovecots gradually ended, and the survivors went free and took to living in towns. There, on buildings everywhere, were ledges which must have reminded them of those on the cliffs where their ancestors had lived and nested. And they were joined by other cousins

– escaped show-birds, and homing pigeons that had failed to complete the return journey to their lofts – to form the great flocks of feral pigeons that we see in every town today.

We not only see the birds. We feed them. Town populations of pigeons depend a great deal on handouts from you and me. So we ought not to complain, I suppose, that having digested that food, they then make messes everywhere, especially on their perching sites. There was one instance where workmen, cleaning a ledge, had to remove a layer of pigeon dung three feet thick! And if statues could come back to life, they wouldn't half complain. Queen Victoria always seems to come off worst, perhaps because there are so many statues of her, perhaps because the birds have got it in for the old girl. The other day I saw her sitting on a throne in the middle of Leeds, and she had a royal faceful of the stuff.

The trouble with pigeon droppings is that they have a corrosive action on stonework, especially limestone. This doesn't make pigeons too popular with town councils, and occasionally efforts are made to cut down their numbers, by destroying nests or offering doped grain. This is wrong, I think, not least because it's a waste of time and energy. Pigeons, like other flock birds such as rooks, seem to have a balancing mechanism that keeps flock size from rising too high. Whether this is controlled by available food supply or fertility or occasional population 'crashes' – say, in a bitter winter – I'm not sure. But overall numbers seem to stay around the same of their own accord. High. Someone has estimated that there are 20,000 pairs of feral pigeons in Inner London alone. And the variety of colour and pattern in the plumage of those 20,000 is, you will find, amazing.

Seeing how many different colours of pigeon you can find is fun. Try it, next time you're sitting in a park or a square (Trafalgar Square best of all). The diversity is huge. But you can pick out three main kinds.

Perhaps the commonest, and certainly the ones that most resemble the wild rock dove, are called 'bars'. They are grey-blue, with a sheen on their necks, a white rump, and two dark bars on the wings. There are more of them in the north of England than the south. The other two kinds are 'velvets', which are plain (in a variety of colours), and 'checkers', which have speckled plumage.

Back in 1971, it was stated that thirty-five species of wild birds bred in Inner London. Very likely that figure's higher now. But there's another figure quoted at that time that I bet is still the same. Of

pigeons in Trafalgar Square

those thirty-five species, there are two that between them make up 88 per cent (almost nine birds in every ten) of the total.

One is the feral pigeon. The other? The house-sparrow.

I'll call the house-sparrow plain 'sparrow' from now on, but be careful not to confuse it with the tree-sparrow. This is a much shyer bird, and different in looks, having a chocolate crown to its head and a double wing-bar. Neither should it be confused with the so-called hedge-sparrow, a name given to the dunnock which isn't a sparrow at all.

The 'house' in its name gives the show away. Sparrows like humans because humans live in houses, and houses provide all sorts of nesting-sites, and also have gardens attached to them, or even farms in the country, where all kinds of things grow that sparrows like to eat. So, not surprisingly, it's a fact that when for some reason men leave a village or an island deserted, the sparrows are the first creatures to go too.

But of course most of Britain's ten million sparrows live in cities and towns, where there are masses of pickings for such bold and busy little birds. Sparrows seem always to be busy, forever on the go in the daylight search for food; and this hard-working approach to life is probably one of the reasons why they are so successful as a species. They don't waste a lot of time in preening and prettying themselves like some birds, though they do like a really good dust-bath, often in the middle of a carefully prepared seed-bed in which you've just sown a neat line of cabbage or carrot seeds. And sparrows, as every gardener knows, can play

sparrows do like a really good dust-bath

havoc with growing plants, and flower-buds too; as with most birds, red is the favourite colour to be attacked, with yellow a close second.

As to singing, sparrows don't, like other birds, sit about singing long complicated songs to proclaim their territories. They don't have to, because they share a territory with all their spadger chums, so there's nothing to make a song about.

This is the point about sparrows – they are the least solitary of birds. They operate in mobs. They are, in truth, mobsters, gangsters, thugs, in fact a kind of bird Mafia, and, in a garden, the sparrow gangs will sweep aside competitors like tits or chaffinches. They are tough guys (who killed Cock Robin?). We think of them, with a certain fondness, as 'cheeky', but other small birds might use 'the sparrow gangs will sweep aside competitors'

different words to describe them if they could: 'selfish', 'noisy', 'mannerless' and 'bullying', for example; especially, perhaps, noisy. Sparrows may not sing but neither do they keep their beaks shut for long, even if all that comes out is that familiar short double-note. Most people think of it as 'cheep-cheep', but once the bird was known as

Philip Sparrow, because that's how some heard it – 'phil-ip, phil-ip'.

Philip or cheep-cheep, sparrow chatter is often the first thing you hear when you wake in the grey dawn, because a favourite roosting or nesting-place is under the eaves of your house. Whoever designed roof-tiles must have been thinking of sparrows, because the shape of the lips is just right for them to sneak in under and begin building their untidy nests in the roof-space, which they start doing as early as March or even February. If they can get right inside buildings – derelict ones, for example – that's even better. You just might be lucky enough to have house-martins nesting under your eaves, building their mud-nests, each with its neat little entrance hole. But the house-martins may not be so lucky, because the gangster sparrows consider those particular nests as very desirable residences, and will take them over, destroying the martins' eggs and young ones to do so.

By the way, if you put up nest-boxes and don't want sparrows as tenants, make sure that the entrance holes are not more than one-and-an-eighth inches in diameter.

Sparrows are finch-like birds, but they aren't true finches; in fact they are related to the tropical

weaver birds, which may explain the shape of their nests, round structures with a side entrance; weaver birds make a beautiful job of theirs, but sparrows, typically, go at it in a slap-happy way, as untidy as can be. They also have a unique habit of occupying their nests in winter, not to produce families but for protection.

The nest itself is made with the stalks of plants, and with straw and feathers and paper. In it, on a thick bed of feathers, the hen sparrow lays between three and eight eggs. Sparrows are faithful birds, sticking to one mate, and the cock bird does his fair share of sitting during the incubation period of about fourteen days. Seventeen days after hatching, the young are fledged, so that at best (or worst) two sparrows could become ten in less than five weeks; and they can have as many as four lots of babies during the six-month breeding season. But a plague of sparrows never actually takes place, because their mortality rate is high.

Perhaps partly because they are so bold and fearless, a sparrow's life expectancy is not long – not much over one year. Man and the motor car and the sparrow-hawk and the kestrel and the cat see to that. And word got round to the tawny owls that there was a plentiful supply of sparrows in town, and the owls moved in from the countryside; as well as sparrows, they take starlings and blackbirds and pigeons.

Sparrows start their courting in February. If I say 'What colour's a sparrow?', you'll say 'Brown'. In fact, a hundred years ago 'sparrows' was a slang word for drinks of beer given to dustmen (all brown, you see – the bird, the beer and the dustmen). But you can easily tell the sexes apart. The male has a black throat or bib, a grey crown and rump, and white wing-bars. The female has none of these and is generally duller in colour.

The courting cock will hop about in front of the

cock sparrows courting a hen

hen, drooping his wings. She may peck at him, apparently uninterested. Then, often, other cock birds arrive until there is quite a pack of them, all wing-drooping away like mad (and of course fighting amongst themselves, another favourite Mafia pursuit). Ornithologists call this a 'sparrow party'. Off flies the hen and the whole lot fly after her, keeping up their courtship till at last she chooses the lucky winner, and the losers hop off.

There's a nice tale in Russian folklore to explain why it is that the sparrow never walks. The story goes that the sparrow is an unwelcome guest because its entry into a cottage means bad luck. So, by some magic, its legs have been for ever tied together by an invisible thread. That's why it can only hop.

Chapter 4

TAKE MY TIP

Humans produce an enormous amount of rubbish. Think of how much stuff goes into your dustbin every week, and then of how many hundreds of thousands of dustbins there must be in a big city. They've all got to be tipped somewhere, and, until the site is full and the bulldozers have buried everything below ground, rubbish dumps attract a host of creatures.

Some, like the fox, may drop in every now and again, but many settle, using the dump as a shelter from severe weather and as protection from predators. Amongst the rubbish there are sure to be things like bits of corrugated iron or asbestos or old tins, which make fine hidey-holes; often these homes have different occupants according to the season of the year – small mammals like voles, for example, in winter, and in summer, lizards or slow-worms and lots of insects.

Many insects, and birds, take advantage of the host of plants that spring up on wasteland. Two of the commonest of these are ragwort and rosebay willowherb, and these are a source of food supply for the caterpillars of moths. The elephant hawk-moth, for instance, will only lay her eggs on the rosebay willowherb. Why? Because it happens to be the only plant that the caterpillars of that species will eat. And at certain times of year, weeds provide a splendid harvest for seed-eating birds, and there is plenty of food too for the insect-eaters in these waste places.

But above all, the rubbish tip is the place for scavenging.

Long ago, the two great scavengers of London Town were the raven and the red kite. The only ravens in London now are in the Tower, and the only kites in Britain are a tiny number that live in a few wooded valleys in the middle of Wales. Don't ask me where exactly. To begin with, I don't know, and if I did, I wouldn't say. Rare birds like the kite, and the osprey in Scotland, are a magnet for those greedy, unscrupulous and, it has to be said, wicked people who will go to any lengths to raid their nests and steal the eggs, and, in the case of birds like the peregrine falcon, to take fledgelings to rear and sell for large sums of money. The fact that all these acts are completely illegal doesn't stop them, and nor does the thought that by doing these things they are making rare birds rarer, and in some cases, bringing extinction dangerously close. So if ever you should be lucky enough to hear, in some remote Welsh valley, a high-pitched call that sounds like 'Hi-hi-heea!' and see above you a soaring bird with narrow, sharp-angled wings and (this is the proof) a long forked tail, enjoy the moment. One day it may not be possible to see such a sight.

The raven and the kite have been replaced in the towns by a host of creatures that find city life agreeable: birds like the pigeon, the starling and the sparrow, mammals like the rat and the mouse, and insects like the cockroach. But the lords of the rubbish dumps are the gulls.

We see a gull of any sort and we think 'a seagull', because we connect the bird with the seaside. But the gull – like the fox – has found out that there are rich pickings in towns. They mainly favour coastal towns but they also come much further inland, especially in the North. A hundred years ago, for

'the lords of the rubbish dumps are the gulls'

example, black-headed gulls were only found – inland, that is – in the Thames estuary. Then in 1946 they began nesting in London. Now they are perhaps the commonest of the gull family to be found in towns everywhere, often nowhere near the sea. Incidentally, black-headed gulls are particularly fond of sewage farms. No accounting for tastes.

In and around Britain the largest populations of this family are of Herring-gulls and the smaller Black-headed. The variety known as the Common

Gull is not particularly common! Others who come to town are the Kittiwake (which cries its name), the Lesser Black-backed gull (which breeds there) and the Great Black-backed (which hasn't – yet).

As with the feral pigeons, the droppings, of the Herring-gull especially, foul ledges and roofs, and someone with a nice sense of humour did a survey in a large, open car park to see which colour of car was bombed most. Blue cars, it was found, received more offerings from gulls than any others. Were they reminded of the sea?

There are a couple of other odd things you might notice about gull behaviour. Small children are not the only ones who like to stamp in puddles, and you may see a gull solemnly marking time in one. It is doing this to encourage worms to surface. And small children aren't the only ones with runny noses either; but if you see a gull's nose running, it's because its kidneys aren't able to cope with the concentrated solution of salt in its digestive system, so this is how it gets rid of it.

Another bird who's always down in the dumps is the starling. The name is supposed to come from an old English word 'staerling' – a little creature that stares – but I don't think much of that. I always fancy it was once 'starveling' – someone 'small children are not the only ones who like to stamp in puddles'

permanently hungry, always on the hunt for food. Like the gull, the starling has only fairly recently discovered the pleasures of city life. Here is a place to find plenty of food; a place which provides a marvellous selection of roosting-places.

Many starlings are residents but, in winter especially, huge numbers come in from the surrounding countryside to spend their nights in warmer, more sheltered dormitories, perching on the thousands of sills and ledges and niches and cornices offered by tall buildings. Large flocks arrive from Russia in winter time too, though curiously they don't join the town birds but take the place of the country commuters. At all events, the net result is that, in any city or large town, you can

starlings

see, at the end of the winter's day, huge flocks of starlings wheeling and swooping and soaring in astonishing displays of mass-formation flying, before dropping down as one bird to perch in their tens of thousands.

Bristol's main railway station has a fine ornamental Victorian façade, and at dusk every nook and cranny of it is plastered with birds, all lit by the lights, all shuffling and settling, all chattering away at the top of their voices. The noise is quite astounding.

There's a certain square in Manchester that is close-planted with parallel avenues of middle-sized trees, trees that on a winter's day might hold nothing more than the odd sparrow. But as night falls, every tree is black with starlings, and you have to shout to make yourself heard.

To a starling, the beauty of a rubbish dump is that it not only provides all kinds of titbits discarded by humans but also, among and often feeding on that waste, numberless insects and grubs. For instance, there is a group of animals (very, very small animals – some clever chap reckoned you could find almost 100,000 of them in one rotten apple) called nematodes. These are roundworms – not related to the earthworm – and they are perhaps the most extraordinary parasites in the world. A parasite, plant or animal, needs another animal or plant as its host, upon which to live and feed, and it's thought that every single species of plant or animal on earth or under water can play host to the nematode (and that includes man).

Many other insects inhabit the dumps and tips

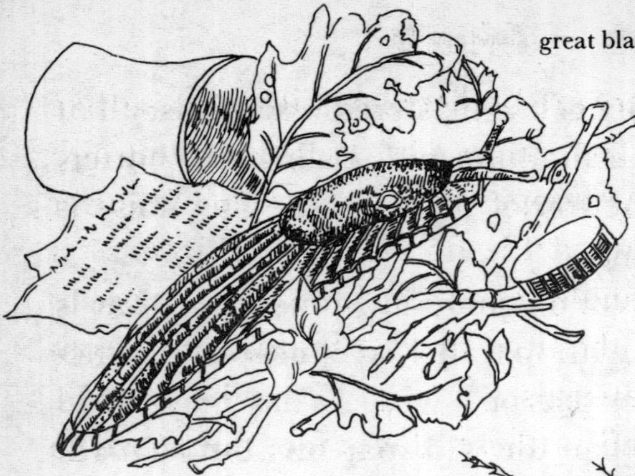

great black slug

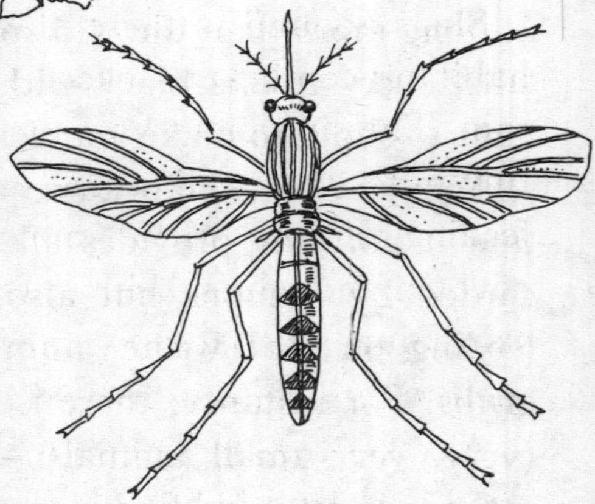

mosquito

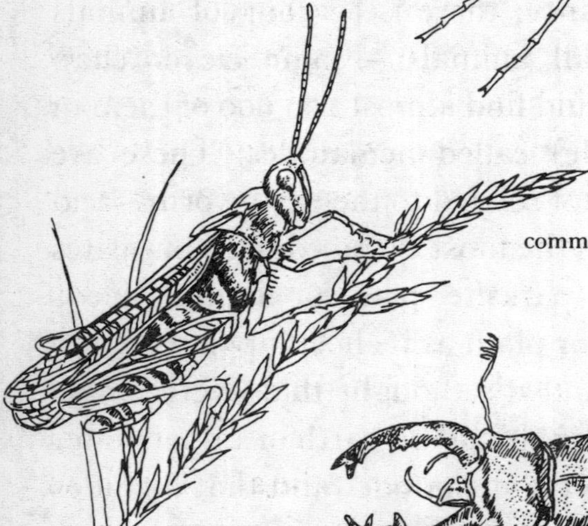

common field grasshopper (male)

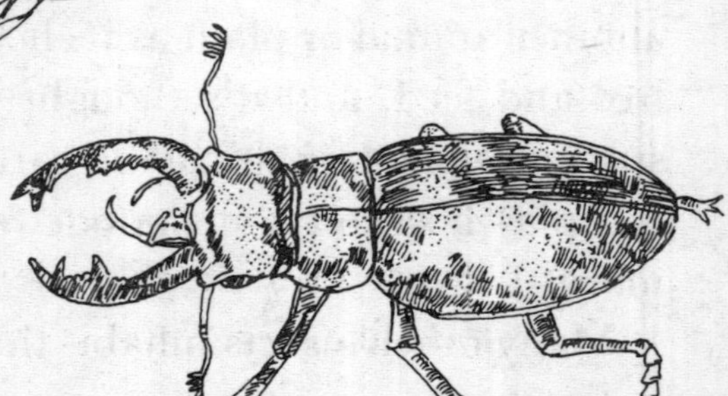

stag beetle (male)

of a town. There are bothersome biting beasts like the gnat and the midge and the mosquito, and there is the grasshopper and the cricket. The latter is properly named the house cricket, because it likes warmth and often takes up residence close to the hearth. In the tip it can get that warmth from fermenting materials.

Slugs abound in these places too, nocturnal in habit but coming out to feed after a good shower of rain. The slug plays host to a number of visitors, tiny mites that walk about on its body, probably feeding on the sticky mucus with which it is covered and which helps it to breathe through its skin. Slugs are hated by gardeners for destroying their plants, but in the tip it doesn't matter.

Also on the tip there are always a number of dead birds and mammals, and this gives plenty of work for two kinds of beetles, the sexton beetle and the burying-beetle, which both live up to their names. In both varieties a pair, working together, will dig a hole and bury the body in it, after which the female will lay her eggs in the corpse. Then, once the larvae hatch, they are surrounded by a tasty supply of putrid flesh.

Another beetle you may see is the stag beetle, so called because of its huge antler-like jaws, which make it look like a creature straight out of science fiction. But it's rather sad, I think, for these fearsome-looking weapons are useless because the muscles which control them are very weak. It's all bluff.

Perhaps the animal for which the rubbish dump seems especially to have been designed is the cockroach. Cockroaches use refuse tips for breeding, for shelter and for food. They'll shelter anywhere, mind you – in your house, if you give them half a chance; and in fact they've been found on the London Underground, riding around in the tube trains.

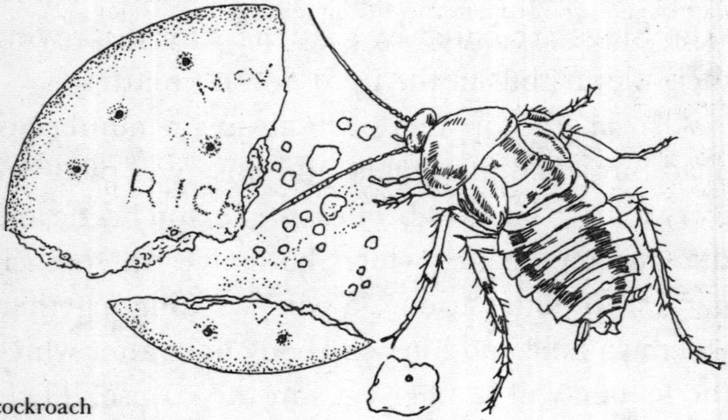

cockroach

The cockroach is such a successful beast because it can feed on almost any kind of material. Whatever it once was, plant or animal, it's all good grub to a cockroach. The more kinds of food you can eat and thrive on, the better your chance of surviving in a competitive world. However, if you're choosy by nature, survival can be a problem, like the koala who only eats a certain kind of eucalyptus leaf which produces special oils, or the giant panda who lives exclusively on bamboo shoots that only grow in certain areas.

The trick is to be omnivorous, to eat any old thing. That's what makes a species successful. Like man. And like that other great survivor, a true scavenger whose tunnels honeycomb every rubbish heap – the rat.

Chapter 5

NOT PETS BUT PESTS

The interesting thing about rats abandoning a sinking ship is not that they certainly would (they are excellent swimmers), but the fact that rats put to sea in the first place.

That's the clue to the worldwide spread of rats: they learned very early that by keeping close to man, they were keeping close to supplies of food, and when men loaded ships with grain and all sorts of other attractive things to eat, the rats went aboard too. And so they colonized the world.

Now, wherever there are people, there are rats, and few animals are so much hated.

The rat's looks are against it: coarse, dirty-looking fur; sharp rodents' teeth; beady eyes; little naked ears and long naked tail. All these turn us against it, and we even see its way of moving – scuttling along, low to the ground – as treacherous and underhand. Yet if the rat's nature was different – if it was gentle and placid, living on greenstuff like a guinea-pig – we would probably regard it in quite another light.

It is precisely because the rat is seen as an enemy to man, spoiling and wasting huge quantities of his food-stores, and fouling and destroying his property, that every man's hand is against it. And no one has forgotten its history of carrying disease, for the fleas borne by infected rats were the cause of the Black Death that killed hundreds of thousands of people in the mid-1300s, and of the Great Plague of London three hundred years later.

The rat is a prime example of a successful species, for two main reasons. First, it is the most prolific breeder. It is because the rat's fertility is so great and its increase so rapid that extermination programmes never quite live up to their name; kill nine out of every ten, and the survivors will soon make up the loss.

The other reason for the rat's success lies in its eating habits. Of all creatures it is the truest omnivore – eater of everything. Not only will it eat anything live that it can catch – nestling birds, swimming ducklings, baby chicks, for example – but anything dead as well, any carrion. Everything it can get its teeth into, the rat will chew, from old boots to electric cables. In addition, it's also a cannibal, polishing off sick or young ones of its own kind. On top of all that, it eats everything that we eat, and where we live closest together – in towns – rats keep as close to us as they can, eat as much as they can, and breed as fast as they can. They become a pest.

Remember them in Browning's poem about Hamelin Town?

> Rats!
> They fought the dogs and killed the cats,
> And bit the babies in the cradles,
> And ate the cheeses out of the vats,
> And licked the soup from the cooks' own ladles,
> Split open the kegs of salted sprats,
> Made nests inside men's Sunday hats,
> And even spoiled the women's chats
> By drowning their speaking
> With shrieking and squeaking
> In fifty different sharps and flats.

We don't have Pied Pipers, but we do have people whose job it is to control pests, and foremost amongst those pests is the rat – in dwelling houses,

'And licked the soup from the cooks' own ladles'

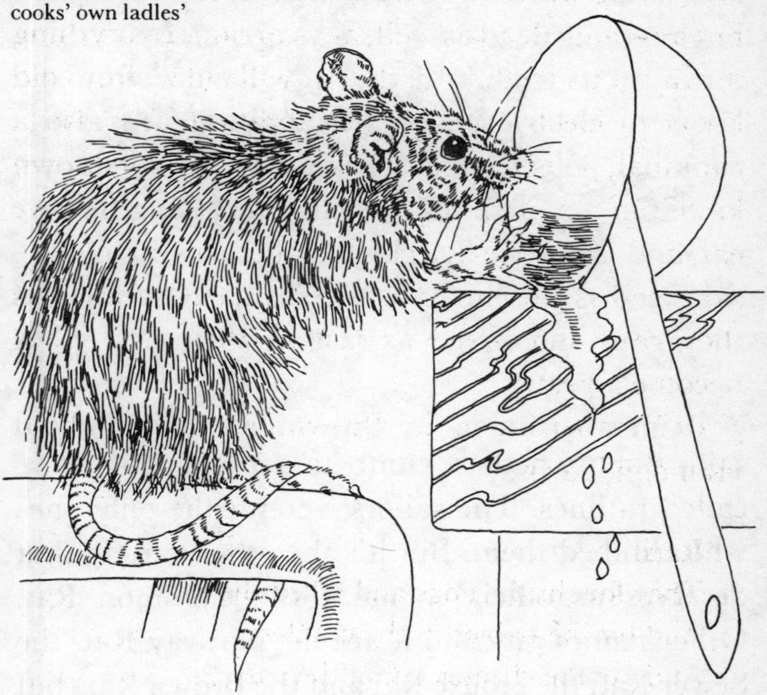

in business premises and factories, on waste ground, in the rubbish tips, in the sewers under the streets.

There are two types of rat, and each variety has several names. The Ship Rat, which is also called the Black, or Roof Rat, is the slightly smaller, slenderer and less common of the two. It is the most expert of climbers, and it's not surprising that the series of rope steps up which the crew of

ship rat

sailing-ships had to climb to set sail aloft were called ratlines. The sailors weren't the only ones who climbed them. But it's the other variety that deserves its official name – the Common Rat. Other names given to it are the Norway Rat, the Sewer Rat, the House Rat and the Brown Rat (but trying to distinguish between the two types by colour is unreliable, since some Common [Brown] rats are blackish and some Ship [Black] rats are brown).

Both varieties have poor sight, and, like many animals, are colour-blind; but both have excellent hearing and a marvellous sense of smell. They have a short lifespan of nine to twelve months, but they don't waste any time while they're alive, for both are capable of producing seven litters in a year, each of eight to twelve babies in the case of the Common Rat, and slightly smaller litters from the Ship Rat.

With reproduction at such a rate, the rat population would obviously assume plague proportions were it not controlled. In the past a variety of traps and poisons were tried, but nowadays the method generally used is much more efficient, and thankfully much more humane. Rats are offered baits of a substance called an anticoagulant, which looks enough like food to attract a rat (who will eat anything, remember) and which the pest control officer lays carefully, to keep it away from children and pets. In a house, for example, he might put a bait behind the cooker, or in the roof-space. The rat eats the bait and becomes unconscious. Then the anticoagulant lives up to its name, for the substance causes internal haemorrhage or bleeding, but the blood refuses to clot, and so the animal dies of that haemorrhage.

It's curious, isn't it? Most of us if asked would say we were fond of animals, but nobody sheds tears over the death of a rat, or of a thousand or a million rats. Probably, if it was announced that the Common Rat had become extinct, we'd all shout hurrah! Yet the domesticated version of the Common Rat, usually white (albino) but also of other colours or with black and white markings, is really a very attractive creature, and makes a most intelligent and interesting companion. At least I think so, on the strength of having kept a couple as pets, of whom I was very fond. But that didn't stop me – when I was a farmer – from killing all the rats that I could, because those rats were in competition with me; they were eating my grain, my cow cake, my pig food, killing my baby chicks, chewing through my electric wiring, and fouling and spoiling everything they touched.

The only 'farm' animals I keep now are three hens to lay me my breakfast eggs. They live in a run under a weeping willow tree in the corner of my garden, and both the pellets on which they are fed and the eggs which they lay are attractive to rats. Some years ago a big doe rat made a home in the compost heap at the back of the hen-house. Sometimes we would see her running along the top of the wall behind it, cheeky thing. When the time came to dig out the compost, I took two of my dogs with me.

The doe escaped, jumping up on to the wall and over to safety, but there were six half-grown youngsters in a tunnel in the compost, and for them there were to be no more meals of my chicken food. I killed one, my German Shepherd a second, and my terrier, quick as lightning, killed three. The sixth young rat dodged us, slipping into the hen-run, but even there there was no escape. The three hens had their revenge for food stolen and eggs eaten, for they surrounded it and pecked at it until I came to finish it off. Rats may be ruthless, but man's more ruthless still.

No prizes for guessing the other common rodent that is not welcome in our homes – the House Mouse. People – some people anyway – tend to think of the mouse differently from the rat, even to have a bit of a soft spot for it, because it's little and nimble and cute and appealing. Anyone in their senses prefers Beatrix Potter's Johnny Town-Mouse to Samuel Whiskers. But once again we don't like mice enough to want them as lodgers, and so we keep cats and set traps and lay poison with a will.

The mouse may be small (weighing half an ounce as against the ten ounces of the Common Rat), but it's just this smallness that fits it to live comfortably in our houses. All of them, especially the old ones, are full of holes and crannies for mice to live in, and useful runways (behind the skirting-boards, under the floors, in cavity walls and roof-spaces) in which they can move freely about.

In houses there are also plenty of nice materials

house mouse

for making nests, and, especially, plenty of good food. Only this morning I climbed the ladder to my loft where I've stored this year's crop from my one apple tree, and found an apple (the biggest and best one, of course) gnawed by sharp little teeth. The toothmarks were much too tiny to have been made by a rat, and, anyway, there were little rod-shaped droppings all around, six times smaller than the pellet-shaped ones of the Common Rat. (The Ship Rat, by the way, leaves spindle-shaped droppings if you fancy playing detective and telling a rat by its dung.)

Back to my apple though – I have to smile when I realize that the fruit is stored directly above my study, directly over my head as I write. Cheeky little devils! But now there is an empty tobacco-tin up there, empty of tobacco, that is, but filled with anticoagulant by ruthless man (me).

The odd few mice in a country cottage are one thing, but it's in the city that the mouse finds its best living. Where there are lots of people, there's plenty of food and shelter and nesting-materials and cosy places to make nests. Mice, like rats, have only a short lifespan, but they can do an awful lot of

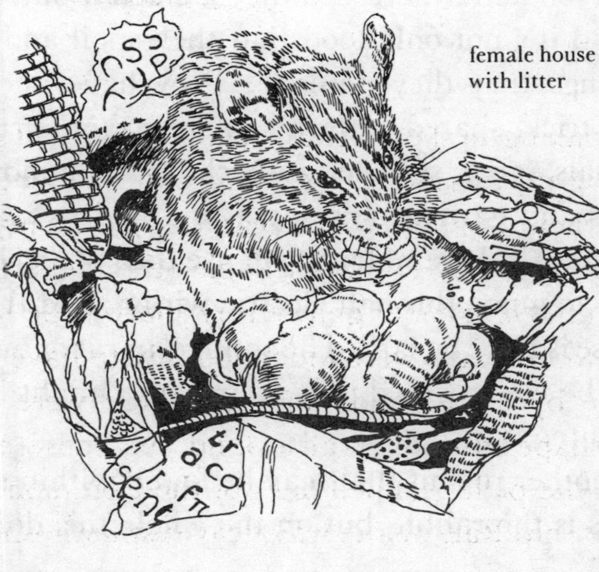

female house mouse with litter

breeding in the time allotted them. They don't have as large litters as rats – usually five or six babies – but they can have them eight times in a year. And mice are sexually mature at six weeks!

They are not great burrowers, like the Common Rat, but prefer to make themselves comfortable inside some kind of stored material, close to, or even consisting of, a store of food. A warehouse, for example, filled with a mountain of grain would be a mouse's idea of heaven, but a nest somewhere near your larder would give it loads of things to nibble at and mess up – biscuits, sugar, butter, cheese, the list is endless. Like rats, mice are poorly sighted and can't distinguish colours, but just leave food anywhere and they'll smell it out.

And it's not only food that they spoil and furnishings that they damage. They have another little trick, shared with rats and some other town animals, grey squirrels, which are common in parks and gardens and often find their way into houses. All these rodents will use their sharp front teeth to gnaw through electric wiring, and this of course is a fire hazard. The squirrel or rat or mouse may be electrocuted, but your house might burn down too.

Another rodent that may be found within town limits is the rabbit, but on the whole this doesn't rate as an urban pest in the way that rats and mice do. Because of myxomatosis, rabbit numbers generally are nothing like what they were, and anyway, rabbits don't invade people's houses. Neither do those city birds I've already mentioned – sparrows and starlings (except under the eaves), or gulls and pigeons. But these last two aren't exactly popular, because of the effect of their droppings on stonework.

All sorts of dodges are tried to dissuade them from perching on ledges and sills, which can be made unattractive to them in several ways: pest control officers use a kind of gel which they squeeze along a sill (rather like piping decorations on top of a cake), which causes an unstable sensation when the bird tried to perch – 'Whoops, this is wobbly,' it thinks. There are also devices made of plastic designed to fit on sills and ledges to stop pigeons landing – miniature beds-of-nails or ranks of sharp-pointed pyramids. But it's a losing battle.

As to control by actually killing the birds, by shooting, let's say, gulls are protected by law; pigeon numbers are generally controlled by the amount of food available, but where the size of the population gets really out of hand due to a glut of food, then action has to be taken. In the port of Bristol, for example, at Avonmouth Docks where there are huge stores of grain and animal feedstuffs, pigeons are shot, as humanely as possible, by trained marksmen using .22 rifles with telescopic sights.

Generally, though, we put up with the town pigeon, regarding it as more pet than pest and often feeding it generously, as you can see in any city square. We treat it thus because it doesn't try to get inside our homes. But insects do, and on those we declare war.

Some, like cockroaches and flies, are disease carriers. Others, such as grain weevils and flour weevils, threaten our foodstuffs. Neither ants nor wasps nor carpet beetles are welcome guests in our homes, nor bedbugs in our beds, nor fleas and lice upon our bodies. All these are attacked without mercy, with liquid sprays and insecticides.

> So, naturalists observe, a flea
> Hath smaller fleas that on him prey;
> And these have smaller fleas to bite 'em,
> And so proceed *ad infinitum*.

So wrote Jonathan Swift a long time ago, but nowadays, the pest officer tries to stop the big fleas from having any little fleas by means of a special hormone preparation which messes up their reproductive cycle. They can still bite but they can't breed. Are you scratching, reading this?

So finally, although living in a town doesn't automatically mean that your house is swarming with rats and mice and bugs, you can see that there are plenty of creatures in every town whom we animal-lovers are only too happy to clobber. We're choosy, you see. We only like certain creatures and we like them to stick to particular places. Like our gardens.

Chapter 6

GARDEN WINGS

Even in the most closely packed cities there are almost always quite large open spaces, like parks or cemeteries or areas of waste ground; but as well as these, nearly every town has a huge number of little islands of open space in which animals live. These islands are our gardens.

Each one is an oasis amidst all the buildings, and each has its own population of living creatures. They range from primitive forms, such as the invertebrates (animals without a backbone – like worms) to highly developed, intelligent beasts like the urban fox, as he drops by to inspect our hen-runs or our rabbit-hutches, or to catch and eat the small creatures that inhabit our shrubberies and flower-beds and vegetable patches and lawns – small rodents, beetles and lots of those old worms.

But the occupants of our gardens that give most people most pleasure are birds. Any kind of garden, however small or uninspiring, will be home to some birds, but just as some houses are more attractive to us than others, so some gardens appeal more to birds because they have more to offer.

The first 'must' is a decently kept lawn, because it makes a fine, open feeding-area. Look out of the window at your lawn and before long you're bound to see a bird on it, searching for food; for grubs, for ants, and of course for worms. There's sure to be a thrush or a blackbird hauling one out of the ground in a one-sided tug-of-war.

These two members of the same family (the blackbird is a kind of thrush) usually work a lawn early, before other birds. 'The early bird catches the worm' is a true saying, because worms like morning dew, not hot sunshine. And another saying which is proved here is 'Might is right', because the blackbird will steal from the smaller song thrush.

You may see either standing still with its head on one side, so that it appears to be listening. In

blackbird

fact it's not, it's looking, because, except for predatory birds like owls where the eyes face forward, the position of the eyes in most birds is on the side of the head – where the human ear is – and the head has to be cocked to one side so that the bird can see its prey.

The blackbird is one of the three commonest British birds (along with the sparrow and the starling), and the sexes are easy to distinguish. The cock bird lives up to his name. He's a glossy black all over, with a bright golden-yellow bill and eye-ring. The hen is a mottled brown. So often this is the case, in birds the world over. Dad, who does the singing and fighting for territory and the showing off to deter rivals and attract mates, is brightly or boldly coloured. Mum, who does the sitting and so does not want to attract attention to herself, is dull feathered. Occasionally you may see a white (albino) or part albino blackbird.

Blackbirds don't walk about as starlings do, but make long, springy hops or run quickly along the ground. Landing from flight, they droop their wings, and raise and fan out their tails.

As a singer, the cock blackbird is superb, better, many people think (and I'm one of them) than the song thrush. Some even rate him above that prince of singers, the nightingale, but I wouldn't agree with that. However, you're unlikely to hear a nightingale in a small town garden, but you're pretty sure to be able to enjoy the blackbird's deliberate, loud and melodious warbling. It takes a lot to stop him singing too. I saw one recently with a mouth full of worms that hung out of either side of his beak as he stopped for a moment on his way to his nestlings, but he was still singing. Rather like the noise a trumpet makes if you put a mute in it, the song was much quieter than usual. The blackbird's notes are purer and flutier than the thrush's, and he doesn't have the thrush's habit of repetition.

There's a famous poem, again by Browning, that says:

That's the wise thrush; he sings each song twice over,
Lest you should think he never could recapture
The first fine careless rapture!

But the blackbird's song seems full of quite different trills and variations; he always seems in his very best voice immediately after a sharp shower of rain.

Song apart, the blackbird makes three other very typical sounds. The first is a screeching chatter, made when suddenly surprised and flushed from cover. The second is a persistent metallic 'tchink-tchink-tchink', used when there's danger about like a prowling cat, or when joining other birds in the daylight mobbing of an owl, and this noise is often also heard at dusk, just before the bird settles for the night. And the third sound is a short warning note which you'll often hear, from both parents, during those anxious first days after their fledgelings have left the nest; for some time the young blackbirds, still unable to fly properly, hop around the garden in a fat and helpless way, fluttering open-beaked before the adults as they beg for food, and generally asking to be eaten by cats or killed by dogs (and often succeeding). 'Tchook!' say the parents urgently, anxiously. It means, 'Keep still!'

A word of warning here. If you find a baby blackbird or thrush (or any fully-feathered youngster that is hopping about on the ground, unable or unwilling to fly, while the parents call their warnings to it), *don't* pick it up. Time and again, well-meaning children think that it is kind to 'rescue' these young birds, and they catch them up and try to feed them, with the best will in the world but the worst results, because only the parent birds can feed their young successfully. Leave the baby alone. Sooner or later (once you're out of the way) the adults will return to it and look after it.

Though the song thrush has a brown back, it's easily told from the hen blackbird because it has a spotted breast. As I've said, the cock thrush's song consists of short phrases repeated ('Did he do it? Did he do it? Judy did.') often as many as four times running, and its alarm call is not 'tchook' like the blackbird's, but 'tchuck' or 'tchick'. The words look much the same when I write them, but the sounds are quite different. And another sound that

the thrush makes is a tap-tap-tapping. If you hear this noise, you'll know that the thrush has picked up a small snail and is bashing it on his 'anvil' – a convenient, often-used stone – to bust its shell.

If you find an old empty nest and wonder if it belonged to a blackbird or thrush, look and see if it has a lining of mud. If it does, it was a thrush's nest. The blackbird makes her nest of grass and rootlets (and mud), but lines it with finer grasses; often it is placed surprisingly low down and none too well hidden. The thrush uses twigs, grass and moss, but lines her nest with mud.

If you find a nest (of any bird) containing

babies, keep well away, so as not to distress the parents; and if there are eggs in it, don't touch, or the mother bird may desert the nest.

One bird you're pretty sure to hear in your garden is the robin. Its song is very clear and high, full of many notes and twitters; a sad song, I always feel, but very sweet. Also it makes two other noises, a long drawn-out 'See-ee', and, when it's angry, at you or the cat perhaps (and robins are very stroppy little birds), a sharp 'Tic-tic-tic!' For the robin also, the lawn is a good place to find food, as it probes with its delicate bill for soft grubs and, again, worms.

Birds' beaks tell you a lot about their preferred food. Soft-billed birds like the robin are insect-eaters. Hard-billed birds such as sparrows and the finches are seed-eaters; their powerful nutcracker beaks can husk corn and other seeds. And many birds have dual-purpose bills, adaptable for hard seeds or soft creepy-crawlies. Finally, birds like hawks and owls that need to tear up the live prey they catch, to eat themselves or to feed to their young, have hooked beaks.

One bird that you'll see on your lawn, the starling, sometimes uses its beak for a very strange purpose. It finds a colony of ants and picks them up one at a time, not to eat them, but to stick them into its plumage, so that eventually there are dozens of angry ants running about amongst the starling's feathers. (Are you scratching again?)

This behaviour, called simply 'anting', isn't really properly understood, but the theory is that what the starling is making use of is a substance called formic acid which ants secrete (and incidentally so do nettles, so the next time you get stung you can comfort yourself by knowing what's causing the pain). The ants, peeved at being used in this fashion, release the acid which then kills tiny feather-mites that have been irritating the bird. Clever, don't you think? The starling is going one better than a bird which, as many do, cleans and conditions its feathers by bathing in water or in dust; it seems actually to have devised a way of ridding itself of a pest by making use of another creature.

Anting is not the starling's only parlour trick. It is also an excellent mimic. As a rule the starling's 'song' is a messy business, consisting of chatters and rattles and clicks and wheezes and chuckles, threaded through with long drawn-out whistles. These are all jumbled up together and delivered in such a busy, jolly way that you can't help feeling the bird's having a lot of fun.

But what is funny to our ears, and maybe to the

starling's, is its power to imitate. There's one in my garden now that's copying exactly the shrill 'Ki-weet!' of a Little Owl. Of the common owls of this country, the Little Owl is most often out and about by day, giving the starling plenty of opportunity to hear its call. But a few years back I heard one of my starlings regularly make the sad, musical cry of a curlew. 'Cour-lee! Cour-lee!' it cried, followed by a typical long bubbling trill. Yet there are no curlews within a hundred miles of my home. Listen carefully next time you see a gang of starlings sitting on a telegraph wire making noises. You may be surprised to recognize the voices of other birds, but you won't be surprised to hear that the starling belongs to the same family as the Indian mina bird. And sometimes, as well as bird noises, you may hear the mew of a cat, the yap of a little dog, or even, as I once did, a word spoken in a human voice.

Some years ago, my next-door neighbour was an old lady called Mrs Jewel. She was a widow, and lived alone with her cat, Timmy, who was the apple of her eye. Cats, unlike dogs, prefer to be out and about in the hours of darkness, but Mrs Jewel could never rest at the end of the day until Timmy was safely inside her cottage. Each evening she would call him from her back door, and if he did not come she would set out to find him. Down the lane at one side of my garden she would go, or through the paddock at the other side, calling his name all the way. Mrs Jewel had a thin high voice and she always called at the same pitch, at intervals of about three seconds. 'Tim-mee! Tim-mee! Tim-mee!' she would cry, the second syllable a couple of notes lower than the first. Then one day Mrs Jewel died, and Timmy went to live with her son in the city, so that plaintive cry was heard no more. That was in the springtime. In the summer I was sitting at my desk writing, when through the open window of my study I suddenly heard once more the ghostly voice of the late Mrs Jewel. At intervals of about three seconds, the second syllable a couple of notes lower than the first, 'Tim-mee! Tim-mee! Tim-mee!' the starling sang.

A surprising variety of kinds of birds will live and thrive in a town garden. Try making a list of those you spot in yours and see how many different sorts you can notch up.

One way to make it easier to do this, and give yourself a lot of pleasure and interest, is to lure the birds to a particular place of your choosing. The lure is food, and the place – a bird-table.

Experts will tell you of all kinds of elaborate structures that you can buy (at great expense), and there is a wide choice of special costly foodstuffs on the market, and of course you can go about it in that way if you want. If you've got a lot of money to spend, you can go and buy, at any garden centre or shop, a rustic monstrosity that looks like a twee little Swiss chalet, and packets and packets of specially mixed bird-food like Swoop, but I think it's better to keep things simple. Make your own bird-table, and as for food, make use first of all of household scraps and oddments from your own larder (first asking permission of the cook), before you start buying stuff.

Here, for what they're worth, are my suggestions for the table itself.

1. Site it where you can see it clearly. Mine, for instance, is just outside my kitchen window, so that I can sit at my breakfast and watch the birds at theirs a few yards away.

2. Design it so as to deny access to unwelcome visitors who may wish to climb on to it and nick the food – cats particularly, but also grey squirrels and indeed foxes. None of this lot can fly, so either build the table on top of a tall (say six-foot high) unclimbable, out-of-cat-jump pole, or suspend it from the branch of a convenient tree.

3. Place it near to cover of some sort – a bush, an ivy-covered wall, a tree – so that birds don't have to make lengthy trips over open ground to reach it. A long flight could mean a short life if there's a sparrow-hawk around.

4. Make the actual table reasonably large. There will be a lot of customers, and if the available space is tiny, only the strongest and boldest will benefit. Build a roof over the platform if you like – it will give you that much more height from which to hang hoppers for seeds or nuts; and have some sort of coaming all round the platform, a couple of

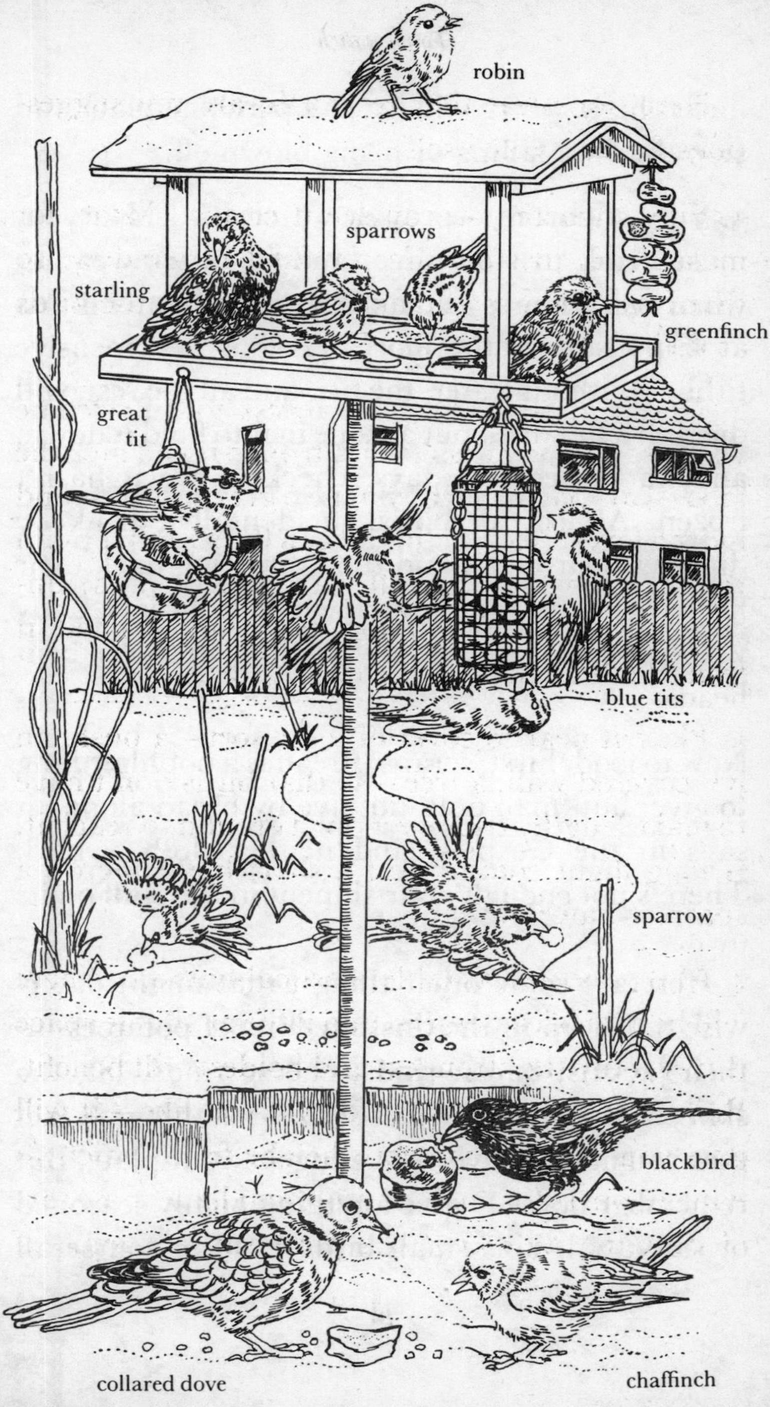
robin
sparrows
starling
greenfinch
great
tit
blue tits
sparrow
blackbird
collared dove
chaffinch

inches high, which will act as a perching place and stop the food falling or being blown off.

5. Very important – provide water. Birds, like you, must drink to stay alive, and in bitter weather when everything's iced up, a supply of water is just as important as the most delicious or expensive titbits. Without water, the tits, and all the rest, will die. Fill a flat dish, put a stone in it to hold it down, and, in the coldest days, check to see it hasn't frozen. Almost all birds, incidentally, drink by dipping their beaks and then throwing back their heads to let the liquid run down their throats. Only woodpigeons can actually suck it up with bent heads.

Now to food. First, scraps. Bread is a popular thing to give, but 'man doth not live by bread alone', it says in the Gospels, and neither doth a bird. There's not enough nourishment in the stuff on its own.

Here are some other things, that might otherwise finish up in the dustbin. Bits of potatoes-in-their-jackets, bacon rinds, cheese rinds, fat, the skin off a ham or a chicken, dozens of things in fact that you might leave on the edge of your plate. But remember never to give anything highly seasoned or salty. Salt kills small birds. And of course all kinds of fruit are good – apples, oranges, tomatoes, bananas. Ask your greengrocer if he'll keep you any that are overripe or in some way unfit for sale. You might turn up your nose at black, soggy bananas but the bird won't turn its beak up.

Porridge oats are popular if you're a porridge-eating family (but not the leftover porridge itself, which will stick to beak and feathers) or if you're cereal people, spare a spoonful of that, dry; the

blue tits

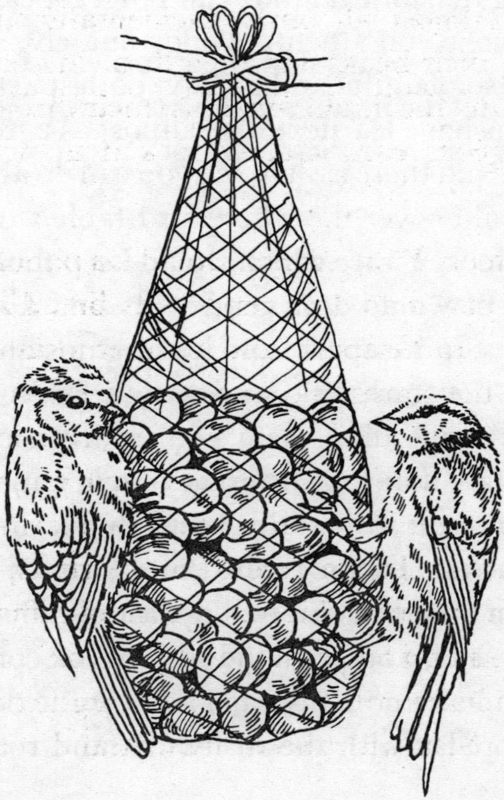

birds won't complain if they can't hear the snap, crackle and pop.

If you decide to go to a shop for bird-food, the best buy is peanuts (not the salted ones). They're full of calories, and you can put them in wire feeding-hoppers and enjoy the sight of great tits and blue tits hanging and swinging on the containers and chipping away at the nuts. Better to feed them like that than loose and whole, because nestling tits, for example, can't digest peanuts and can choke on them. Unfortunately, because they're so plentiful and greedy, both sparrows and starlings have learned to be almost as acrobatic as the tits, and there isn't much you can do about this. You could cover the whole bird-table with small-mesh chicken-wire which would keep the starlings out but it would also deprive the blackbirds and thrushes, quite apart from looking unsightly. I try to take the starlings' minds – and beaks – off the table by providing them with a diversion, a big lump of fat that I get from the butcher and hang in a nearby tree; at least this keeps the starlings away from the table some of the time.

Other good seeds to buy are sunflower and canary seed, and any kind of corn. Coconuts (cut them in half and hang each half upside down) are very popular with the tit family, and robins love mealworms. Mealworms are the larvae of a beetle called Tenebrio that breeds in granaries and flour-stores. You can buy them from pet-shops or suppliers of bird-food, or you can breed them yourself if you like.

To do this, get an old biscuit tin, punch some holes in the top for ventilation, and put a bit of sacking in the bottom; put a layer of corn on the sacking with bits of bread, potatoes, cabbage, carrot or apple; then more sacking and another layer; then do it a third time. Now you've got a three-tier sandwich.

Buy two or three hundred mealworms and pop them in. The worms will turn into pupae which turn into little black beetles which will lay eggs which will turn into mealworms!

The main thing to remember is that the food you put out must be varied, because the birds that will come to it have different eating habits. Some are carnivores, some vegetarian, some eat anything; some are seed-eaters, some insect-eaters. But keeping a well-stocked bird-table is above all an act of conservation. From late spring right through the summer till late autumn, there is no need to provide food. Forget your bird-table in these months. The birds will find plenty of natural food. But in the winter, especially in the coldest weather, a bird can lose a lot of its body-weight overnight, and it needs to make up that loss during the comparatively short daylight hours, with good nourishing food (and don't forget that water). A small bird, even if it's perfectly healthy, can die in a couple of hours in severe weather, and it's not the cold that kills it. It's lack of food.

There are many birds which, because of their habits and lifestyles, you cannot reasonably expect to see in a town garden. Birds of moor and mountain, birds of estuary and foreshore (apart of course from all those visiting gulls), the shyer woodland birds, and rarities which can only be seen in certain tracts of the countryside. Mind you, funny things do sometimes happen if you keep your eyes skinned. I was sitting in a town garden once with a group of friends when someone looked up into the sky and said, 'Whatever's that?' We all looked up, and there was this huge white bird, four or five feet long, solemnly flapping along behind its enormous beak. It was a pelican, escaped from the zoo!

But there is, as I've said, a surprising variety of birds that you may well see in your garden if you live in a city or a town. Some I've already mentioned. Here are a number of others, some of which you're pretty certain to see, and some that you might if you're lucky.

From the crow family – the jackdaw, the magpie, the jay and the carrion crow itself.

From the pigeons – the woodpigeon and the collared dove.

From the woodpeckers – the green and the great spotted.

From the finch family – the greenfinch, the chaffinch, the goldfinch and the bullfinch.

As well as the song thrush – the much larger, heavily spotted mistle thrush.

As well as the great and the blue tit – the coal-tit and perhaps the long-tailed tit.

Others that spring to mind are the pied wagtail, the spotted flycatcher, the tree creeper and the whitethroat; and if you're lucky and live in a house whose roof has overhanging eaves, you could have swallows or house-martins nesting under them.

While we're on the subject of nesting, you may want to help the birds in your garden by providing nest-boxes. If you do, remember three things. Put them up at the end of February. Put them where cats can't reach them. And don't put them too close together, but allow plenty of territorial space between them.

There are probably lots more kinds of birds that you may see, and you could be lucky and spot something very rare and unusual (like a pelican!); and I've just remembered that I haven't even mentioned two of my favourites – the dunnock and the wren.

But for me – as for a lot of people – top of the pops is the robin. My grandmother was crazy about robins. She probably knew the fable that the robin was once just a dull brown bird until, on an impulse of compassion, it plucked a thorn from the crown that Jesus wore upon the cross, and wounded itself, so that, from that moment on, its breast was blood-red. She would doubtless have known that in Victorian days postmen were called 'robins' because they wore red waistcoats. And she would certainly have given and received umpteen Christmas cards with robins on them.

But I don't think she did know (and she wouldn't have believed it if she'd been told) that the robin is actually an extremely aggressive, unsociable little bird, only putting up with the company of its own mate long enough for breeding, and fiercely protecting its chosen territory against other robins, its head well up in a hostile display to show that red breast.

However, there are several things that endear the robin to me and all robin-lovers. One is its strange choice of nest-sites – on a shelf in an

robin's nest

outhouse, inside an old discarded bucket or kettle, or even, as I was once shown, inside the pocket of an old coat that hung in a shed. Another is its apparent friendliness (which is really, I suppose, a lack of fear) as it follows me closely as I dig in the garden and turn up the worms and grubs and insects upon which it feeds; and if I drive the spade into the earth and walk away, you can bet your life that in two ticks the robin will come and perch on the handle.

But best of all is its song. The robin is not a great singer like the blackbird or the nightingale, but its song is very sweet and clear and high, a varied series of short warbling phrases; and the joy of it is that you can hear it when there is no other sound of song. All the year round, even in the shortest darkest days when all the other birds are silent, you can be sure of hearing the robin's song. Reward it. Put some mealworms on your bird-table.

Chapter 7

GARDEN THINGS

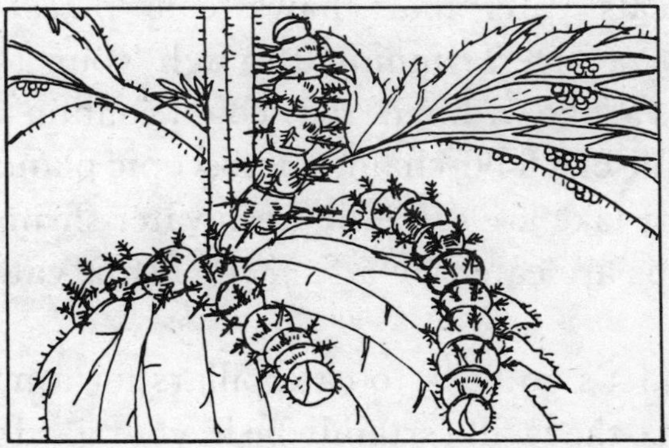

Birds are by no means the only creatures which you may see in a garden in the heart of a town. They are perhaps the most obvious, because their flight catches the eye and their song pleases the ear, and because they live so closely with us, often with little fear of man. But there are lots of other animals about.

For a start, there are all the insects and grubs that many of those birds feed on (remember incidentally that searching for food takes up a very large part of many animals' days). A caterpillar is a good example of a creature that forms part of what is called a food-chain, where a plant-eating animal (a herbivore) is eaten by a flesh-eating animal (a carnivore), who may in turn be eaten by a larger carnivore. That particular food-chain would start with a leaf: caterpillar eats leaf; blackbird eats caterpillar; hawk eats blackbird. If there's a river running through your town or there's a lake within it, they could contain another example of a food-chain: microscopic plants in the river or lake are eaten by freshwater shrimps; the shrimps are eaten by a fish; the fish is eaten by a heron.

But let's go back to caterpillars for a moment, because they will certainly be in your garden (and not very welcome if they're the kind that chews a lattice-work of holes in your cabbage-leaves), and some of them will eventually become beautiful butterflies. The kind you're most likely to see is the Small Tortoiseshell (the Large Tortoiseshell is rare), and the next common is probably the Peacock that has lovely 'eyes' on its wings, just as its namesake bird has on its tail-feathers. Then there is the brilliant Red Admiral that you'll certainly see if you have a pear tree or a plum tree, for it will come to suck the overripe windfalls. And you may see a Painted Lady, and perhaps a Comma with its elegantly sculptured wing-edges; and of course there's the Large White, which some call the Cabbage White and we know why.

Earliest of all in the spring is the Brimstone, and for me it's always a thrilling sight to see the first bright-yellow male dancing his way across the flower-beds. My grandfather had a huge collection of butterflies and moths. He was the kindest, gentlest man, and I'm sure it never occurred to him that there was anything wrong with catching a beautiful butterfly in his net, and gassing it in his killing-bottle, and mounting it with a pin on one of the hundreds of setting-trays in his collection. I didn't see anything wrong with it at the time either (I was about ten on the day which I'm remembering), and when he said we would go on an expedition to try to catch a particular sort of butterfly, I was all for it.

We drove all the way to Dorset, to a place called Lulworth Cove, because there we hoped to find a little brown butterfly called the Lulworth Skipper. It took us an awful long time to get there because my grandfather never drove faster than about twenty-five miles an hour, and then we searched for another awfully long time and found nothing. Then, at the last moment, just as we were about to give up, a little brown butterfly flew up from the grass in front of me and flittered away, and away I rushed after it and caught it in my net, and it was a Lulworth Skipper!

tortoiseshell

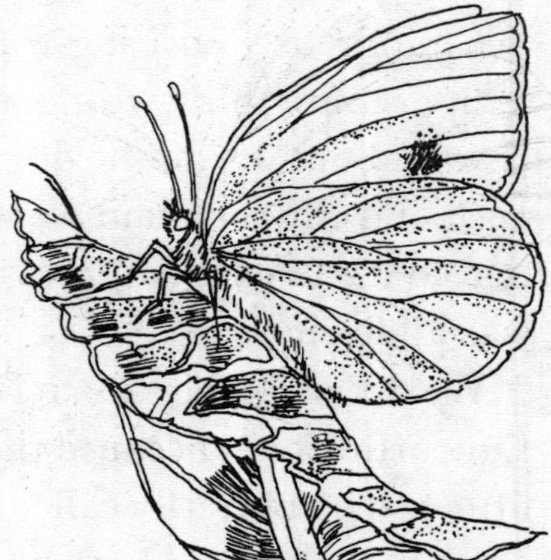

large white

peacock

painted lady

brimstone

red admiral

But now I hope you're not a butterfly collector. Butterflies have such short lives anyway. I'd much rather you tried to attract them to your garden just to admire them, and one way to bring them in is to keep a wild bit of the garden specially for them. Gardeners, I know, like to have everything neat and tidy, and must wage continual war on weeds; but try, for example, to have a clump of nettles somewhere in an odd corner. They will attract butterflies. The trouble with flowers like chrysanthemums and dahlias is that they produce very little nectar, so insects don't like them. But if you have some valerian growing on your walls or some buddleia in your wild garden, they will bring the butterflies flocking when they flower.

Everybody's garden is actually heaving with insects, and the great majority are solitary animals; that is to say, they take absolutely no interest in one another except during the very short period of mating. But there are a number of social insects too. The definition of a social insect is that the female continues to have contact with her eggs after she's laid them, and with her young after they've hatched. Ants, bees and wasps are all social insects, and perhaps the life of the honey-bee is the best known. But I want to tell you a little about one of my favourites, the bumblebee.

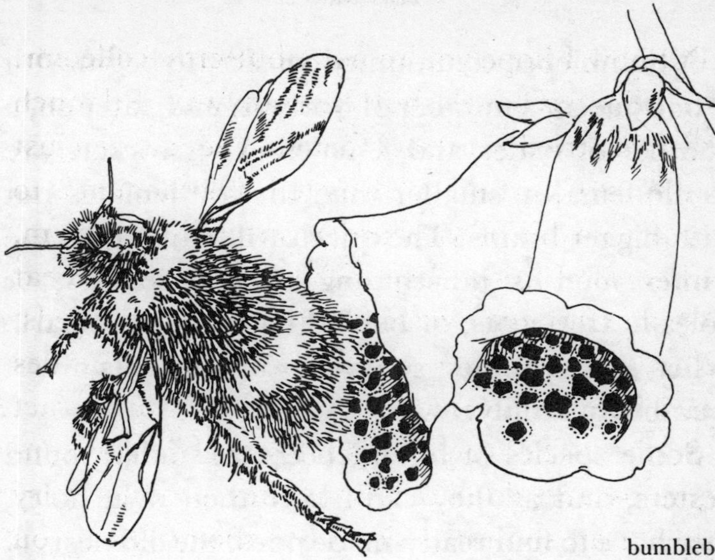

bumblebee

I suppose I like it because it's large and fat and hairy and makes such a comfortable booming noise as it flies around in a rather slow and dignified way, like a tubby, old-fashioned airliner. Sometimes it's called the humblebee (from the German word *hummel* – the buzzing bee), but I think its nicest name is a dialect one – the dumbledore. By the way, bumblebees can sting. One day years ago one got into the kitchen and as I went to catch it in my hand to put it out in the garden, everybody said, 'Watch out! It'll sting you.'

'Rubbish,' I said. 'Bumblebees don't sting.' Yeeeeow!

A bumblebee community consists to begin with of one queen, a number of workers, and, later on, a number of males and females. The workers are sterile females, smaller than the full females but with bigger brains. The queen will have spent the winter months hibernating, in mouseholes, or holes in tree-roots, or behind loose strips of bark. When spring comes, she wakes up and sets about founding a family.

Some species of bumblebees are underground nesters, and as they can't bore their own holes, they have to find ready-made ones; the old nests of fieldmice are a popular choice, but if you want to attract bumblebees to nest in your garden, just bore a hole about a foot deep, at an angle of around thirty degrees, and leave a bit of nesting material nearby.

Other bumblebees are ground nesters, making their nests on the surface in thick grass or other plants (periwinkle is a favourite), or amongst ivy. They are called carder-bees. The nest is usually made of dead grass and moss woven together, looking like the nest of a small bird, and in it the queen builds a little round nut-sized pot of wax and pollen. In this she lays about a dozen eggs. Then she seals it up. She goes on to build a lot more pots, some to hold more eggs, some to store honey in. About three weeks after the first eggs have been laid, the first of the season's bumblebees hatch out, and they are all workers; skilled housemaids and baby-sitters who start straightaway to help their mother. As more workers appear, so the queen is excused housework altogether and can concentrate on laying eggs.

Towards the end of the season males and females are born and before long, these fly out and mate. Then the fertilized females (who will be next season's queens) find a nice place to hibernate. They're the lucky ones. The males die after mating, and the poor old workers, after all that effort helping mum, are killed by the cold as the nights draw in.

Another fascinating social community is that of wasps. Mind you, I'm not all that keen on wasps, I have to say. In late summer, when my plums are ripening, it's war between me and the wasps. My weapons are jam jars filled with a mixture of sugar and jam and golden syrup and home-made wine, in which they die a glorious drunken death by drowning, and theirs are their stings. But though I don't like them much, I do admire their skills.

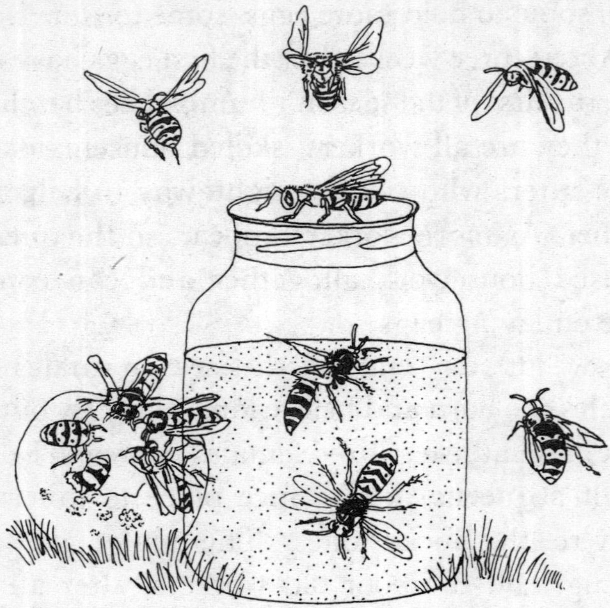

'in late summer, when my plums are ripening, it's war between me and the wasps'

Wasp communities operate in much the same way as the bumblebees, except in the matter of nest construction. Wasps have no wax, so they make their nests of paper. But first they have to make the paper. This always intrigues me, because I come from a family of papermakers, and the wasps make the paper that they need from wood-pulp, in much the same way as my grandfather and my father and my brother all did.

The queen scrapes off very fine shavings of wood from fence-posts and the walls of garden sheds and similar places, and makes them into paper with her own saliva (my family used water!). The nest starts as a flat sheet of paper with a lot of six-sided cells hanging down from it. The queen lays one egg in each cell.

From now on – until the first larvae emerge as workers in a month's time – the queen wasp has a hell of a life. She has to find food for the larvae, which means not only catching masses of caterpillars and flies and other insects but also chewing them up to feed to the grubs. She has to enlarge their cells as they grow in size, and, if the nest is in a hole in a bank or under a shrub, has to excavate more and more soil from it to allow for the increasing bulk of the nest as she builds more cells and lays more eggs to fill them. Only when the first workers emerge to help, can she take things a bit easier, like the bumblebee queen; and devote her time purely to egg-laying.

When the workers get cracking, the nest really begins to grow like mad. And these papermakers build with superb skill, making layer upon layer of paper 'comb' – successive horizontal platforms along which the wasps can walk – until by the beginning of August the whole thing is as big as a football.

Once again, nearly everyone dies as winter

approaches. The males, their job done, come to the end of their short lives, and the workers destroy the unhatched eggs, stop feeding the remaining larvae, and soon, in company with the old queen, die themselves of starvation and cold. All the hard work, all the amazing expertise, all the dedication leave nothing at the end but a few fertilized females to start the whole process up again in the coming year.

I could go on and on about the insects you could find in a town garden – I haven't even mentioned spiders yet, or indeed ants, the most highly developed and successful of all social insects and, in fact, the dominant insects of the world – but I must find room for another favourite, the ladybird.

These little one-third of an inch beetles, brightly coloured and attractive, are actually voracious carnivores, and their prey, food for both adults and larvae, is the aphid or greenfly. Greenfly do a lot of damage to plants, so the ladybird really is the gardener's friend and he should welcome the hibernating groups he may find in his shed, knowing how much they will help him in the growing season, when they will lay their eggs as near as possible to an aphid colony.

A fortnight after a ladybird larva has hatched from its egg, it will become inactive. Then its skin will split to reveal the pupa, which looks like a

small bird-dropping. Ten days later the pupal skin splits and out comes the adult beetle. Seeing how many different varieties of markings on ladybirds you can find is fun. There are the 2-spots, some with red spots on a black background, some with black spots on a red background; sometimes this type, despite its name, carries four spots or up to six, and all these can interbreed. Then there's the 7-spot; and the 10-spot; and finally a small, neat variety that has twenty-two black spots on a yellow background.

See how many you can spot!

Another creature that will appreciate a bit of wild garden is the grass snake. I can never understand why people don't like snakes. They think them slimy and cold, which they're not, and somehow evil, so that their reaction on seeing one is either to run or to kill it. But the grass snake is completely harmless. The worst it can do is to exude a rather nasty-smelling slime if you pick it up. So don't; but don't hurt it either. It is easy to recognize, being dark brown or green on top, and having a yellow or white collar and jaws, and yellow eyes. Males average three feet in length, females four, and grass snakes, incidentally, are excellent swimmers. But should you by any chance come across a snake that resembles the grass

adder(or viper)
grass snake

snake, though a little smaller, but has a central black zigzag line running the length of its back and coppery red eyes, don't on any account pick that one up. It will be an adder (or viper), and it's Britain's only poisonous snake. The poison is not as lethal as that of foreign snakes like cobras or rattlers or mambas, but a bite can make people feel quite ill, and can, very occasionally, cause death. However, you're most unlikely to meet an adder in a town garden.

You just might meet a slow-worm though, which looks like a small (foot-long) snake but is actually a legless lizard. It's completely harmless,

the slow-worm can snap off its tail by a muscular contraction

but it does have one rather clever trick. Its only defence against an enemy, such as the hedgehog which likes to eat snakes, is to snap off its tail by a muscular contraction. The snapped-off tail wriggles and jumps about like mad, attracting the hedgehog's attention – or that's the idea! – while a rather shorter slow-worm slides (slowly) away.

The largest snake I've ever handled was a python called Eric. Eric was ten feet long (quite small for a python), and I carried him, wrapped around my shoulders and generally all over me, for the best part of an hour; I had to have lots of rest in between because he weighed half a hundredweight.

Pythons kill their prey by throttling it to death before swallowing it whole. They can unhinge their jaws, thus opening them wide enough to take in unbelievably large animals. And of course Eric could have given me a very nasty bite even if he didn't go any further. Luckily I didn't have to worry about this, because Eric was very used to being handled, since his keeper (who was never far away) took him regularly to schools to show him to children.

I could simply enjoy the unforgettable experience of being in such close contact with so fascinating an animal. To see, and feel, the thousands of muscles rippling and moving under that beautifully marked, warm, dry skin, and to guess at the power within Eric's body, was thrilling. Only once towards the end of our time together, when perhaps he was getting a bit bored with me, did he start, very gently, to squeeze my neck. I thought that was a good moment to hand him over to his keeper.

If there's a pond in your garden, then you're that much more likely to see a grass snake, for frogs are its favourite food. The French may only eat frogs' legs but the grass snake eats the lot. (Incidentally, here's a nice food-chain: worm is eaten by frog which is eaten by grass snake which is eaten by hedgehog which is eaten by badger.)

Personally I'd prefer a toad (not to eat but to have in my garden!). Toads are most unfairly disliked and cast in myth as a beast of the witch or even the Devil. Possibly this is because they are slightly venomous to other animals, being able to exude a mild poison from the warts on their bodies as a defence, or perhaps it's because they're considered ugly. I don't think they are. I think the toad is a most attractive creature, and certainly it's a friend to any gardener. It has an excellent sense of direction, and though it may go foraging quite a long way for food – it has the most insatiable appetite for woodlice, worms, snails, ants, caterpillars and lots of other insects – it will return to its chosen home, a hole in a wall perhaps, in your garden and live with you for ages. One naturalist recorded that a particular toad lived under the doorstep of his house for thirty-six years. If you

toad

want to do some toad-spotting, the best time to look is late evening or early in the night, though they will come out in daylight during a heavy shower.

Go out at dusk on any really warm evening from April onwards and you'll have a good chance of

pipistrelle bat

seeing a bat. Most likely it will be the commonest kind, the Pipistrelle (which country people sometimes call the flittermouse), a little bat with a wing-span of about eight inches, the span of a man's hand from thumb to little finger. You may hear it (children, and adults with particularly sensitive hearing, sometimes can) making its high, shrill, squeaking call. Usually it will fly on a regular beat, round a tree or a building, dodging and twisting as it takes insects on the wing. The Pipistrelle is a very useful insect-killer. It has to be

on a warm evening from April onwards you'll have a good chance of seeing a bat

– each individual needs to catch about three thousand insects every night! And they can detect a flying insect less than half an inch across by means of their amazing echo-locating system. This is what the continual series of high-pitched squeaks that each bat makes when hunting is all about. It's a kind of natural radar, because the sounds echo off anything that they hit, and the bat's ears pick up these echoes. Thus they can build up a 'sound picture' of everything around them.

Like the toad, bats have always been portrayed as demons and evil creatures, and silly stories are told about them getting tangled in people's hair. They're certainly not the prettiest of beasts to our eyes, and they are very smelly, but I think we should forgive them these faults and simply marvel at their quite amazing skills in direction-finding. Bats, incidentally, are protected animals. I can't imagine that people who are lucky enough to have a colony of these fascinating beasts living in their roof-space would wish to be rid of them. But if they did want to, they could only do so with special permission.

If you're really lucky, you could have a hedgehog as tenant of your town garden. It may wander a lot, but if you provide it with regular food at a particular place, it will treat your territory as its base. But remember that there are hedgehog death-traps in some gardens. One of the worst, which you're most unlikely to have in town, is a cattle-grid. Hedgehogs get in but can't get out again. Luckily, there's a special society that looks after the interests of hedgehogs, and, thanks to a campaign by them, responsible people now build in a ramp when they are constructing a cattle-grid. Hedgehogs that topple in are thus saved from either starving to death in this dungeon, or often, drowning in it when it becomes water-filled. And you may well not have a tennis-net, in which the animals can get stuck, but you could have a pond and if you do, it's a good idea to make a scrambling-net out of chicken-wire, so that a hedgehog that falls in will be saved from drowning. But the worst hazard for your hedgehog is something that many gardeners use – slug pellets; put them in a narrow pipe and only the slugs will die.

People traditionally give hedgehogs a saucer of bread and milk. They'll eat this, but must, I should think, find such a diet extremely boring. (You'll know that any saucerful of food you provide has been eaten by a hedgehog and not by something else, if the saucer is tipped over. Its meal finished, the hedgehog automatically tips the dish over on the offchance of something like a worm hiding underneath it.)

But hedgehogs really like something a bit more solid, preferably tinned dog-meat or tinned salmon. So keep your cat or dog indoors at hedgehog feeding time – around about dusk, from late March till November. There's no need to look for your tenant in the winter because it will be hibernating, probably under a pile of leaves. (Be careful if

you're lighting a bonfire. There could be a tragedy.)

It's possible, I understand, to get a hedgehog so accustomed to your feeding ritual and your presence that it will actually come and take a titbit like a mealworm from your hand. What's more, your hedgehog will earn its keep. It eats masses of the gardener's enemies like slugs and caterpillars, but doesn't, for example, eat ladybirds, which gardeners like because they in their turn eat greenfly.

Just how many different types of animals you may see in a garden in town depends of course on size and location, but there's a whole list of creatures that I haven't even mentioned yet that could be within your boundaries, even if you've never clapped eyes on them.

There's the mole that ruins your lawn, the fox that raids your dustbin, a crowd of small rodents like fieldmice and voles and shrews, and the weasel and the stoat who prey upon them, and even perhaps the largest of all the weasel family, the badger.

Chapter 8

IN THE CHURCHYARD AND THE PARK

Though we've grown used to thinking of the fox as not only an animal of the woods and fields, but also of the city and town, we still tend to think of the badger as a completely rural beast, living deep in the heart of the countryside. Yet, at the last count I can find, there were twenty-five badger setts (and that could mean a great many badgers) actually within the boundaries of the city of Bristol. That survey was done ten years ago, but I would guess that numbers since then have, if anything, risen.

Maybe Bristol is not a typical city to choose, because it does have a large green belt in the shape of the Clifton Downs, but even so, it is quite proper to think of the badger as an animal of town as well as country.

To some extent it has made the move for the same reasons as the urban fox – to make use of man's leavings and to make its home in the various open spaces with which any town is dotted; but generally it's not so much a case of badgers coming to town as of the town coming to the badgers. A built-up area expands, a new road is cut, a housing estate mushrooms, and what was wide-open badger-country where the animals may have lived for centuries, suddenly becomes closed-in man-land. If it is at all possible (and they survive the invasion), the badgers will stay despite the changes happening around them. They seem to have a strong sense of belonging to a traditional locality, and, unlike the footloose fox, they will cling on to their old chosen places as long as they can.

So there are plenty of records of displaced badgers digging new setts very close to houses, for instance, under garden sheds, and certainly railway embankments are popular sites, resulting, alas, in many badgers being killed by trains or electrocuted. Many more are killed on the roads, especially during the months of February, March

railway embankments are popular sites for badger setts

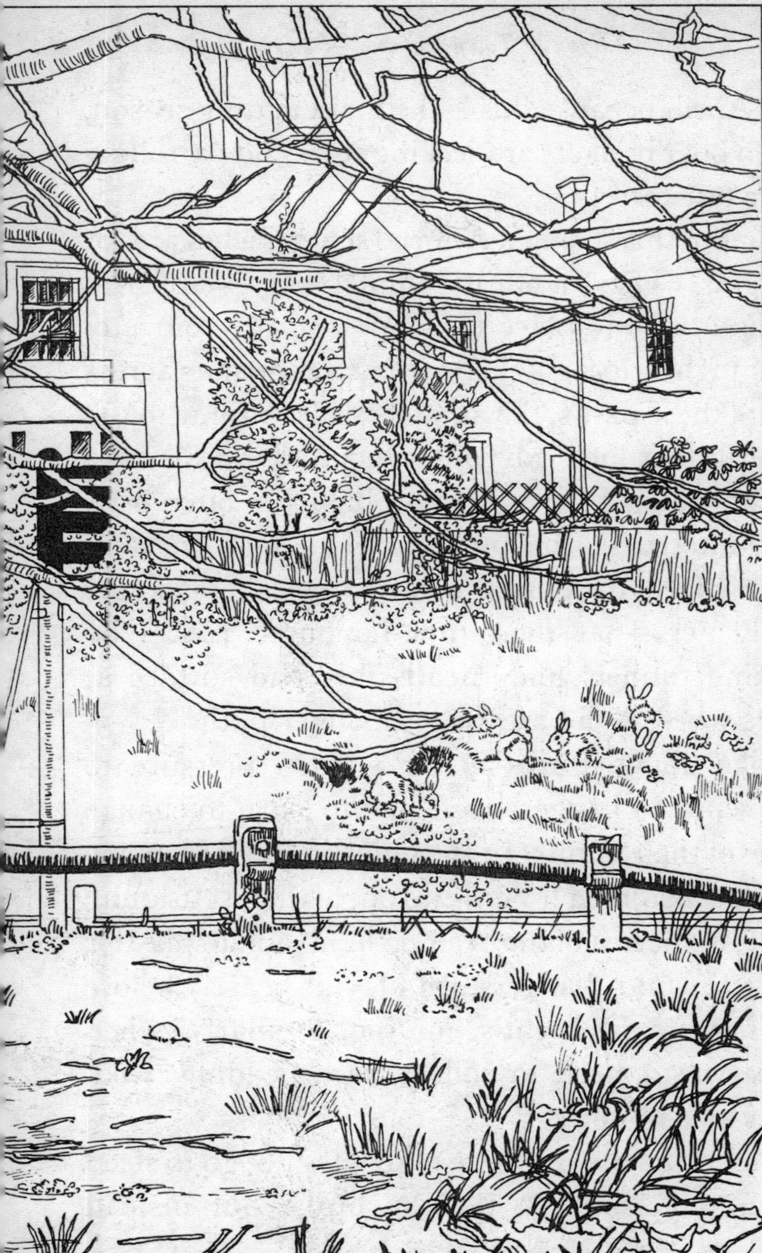

and April, because this is the main mating season, when boar badgers are seeking sows and patrolling their territories.

Again, this strong territorial sense is a hazard for badgers. They tend to follow long-established paths from one place to another in the course of their nightly foraging; and if a new road cuts across one of these paths, the animals will continue to use it – till their luck runs out. On a larger scale, and mainly outside towns, this problem has often been encountered in the building of motorways, and some efforts have been made to help badgers get safely across at their time-honoured places by making tunnels underneath the road surface at spots where there are known badger-paths.

Like all creatures under sudden pressure to evolve, town badgers have had to learn to change some of their habits. In the quiet countryside, they were accustomed to come up out of their setts quite early, in the last of the evening light, and to play for quite a while (badgers are playful beasts) before leaving for the night's hunting. Similarly, when there was a need to collect fresh bedding, well, there was no hurry.

But in the town, where man does not go to sleep when it gets dark, like the birds, but instead switches on lights everywhere and wanders about with dogs and drives around in cars, the badgers have had to change their ways. Bedding collection is only done during the longer nights, and town badgers emerge from their setts much later and don't play for as long, but go straight off on the night's foraging.

Areas like railway embankments, quiet and undisturbed (if you don't count the trains, to the noise of which animals become very accustomed), are occupied by many other creatures besides badgers, for example rabbits.

Before the onslaught of myxomatosis in 1953, the number of rabbits in Britain was so enormous that many town colonies had already been formed. Now, despite the astonishing fact that the disease is reckoned to have killed sixty million rabbits (a larger number than there are people in the British Isles), pockets of resistant animals have survived, and the railway bank is a nice deserted place for digging burrows. Sometimes those burrows are taken over and enlarged by foxes, for the embankment is home to a variety of small rodents which make excellent fox-food.

Some other places in town that are much favoured by mice and voles and shrews are

field vole

churchyards and cemeteries. Quiet and undisturbed and often supplying a plentiful cover of tall grasses, they provide splendid territory for many small mammals who construct regular runways among the grass stems. Common Shrews make a maze of tunnels, but Pygmy Shrews are lazier and either make use of their larger cousins' tunnels or of those made by voles.

shrew

Shrews are amazing little beasts (and 'little' is the word – the Pygmy Shrew is only about three and a half inches long, almost half of which is tail, and weighs no more than a fifth of an ounce). Very few shrews survive more than a year, so that they only see one breeding season when each family may have two litters, in spring and in summer, of five to ten young in a ball-shaped nest of grass under a log or a root. But many mothers will die before their young are weaned, because of the number and variety of predators that shrews have to face.

Owls, kestrels, stoats, weasels and moles all kill and devour shrews, but cats and dogs, though they will kill them, won't eat them, probably because of the musk glands that every shrew carries on its flanks that make it smell, and taste, pretty nasty. The shrew's real problem is that it needs to be forever searching for food; without food it can die in a few hours, and it's capable of eating four times its own weight in a day and a half. So it's constantly foraging day and night with only very brief shrew-naps in between, and therefore constantly at risk from enemies.

Shrews are not only ravenous but very fierce little animals, and will fight to the death amongst themselves. If your hearing is good enough, you could catch the sound of their high furious squeals. Curiously, when the shrew tackles its own prey, it produces a poison mixed in with its saliva, so that by injecting this it can control something large (say, the young of a ground-nesting bird) which it might not otherwise have been able to subdue.

As well as shrews, voles find churchyards attractive places. There's no confusing the long-snouted shrew with the far larger vole which has a blunt face and a plump body. You may just hear the Bank Vole which spends much of its time in underground tunnels, but you're more likely to see the Field (or Short-tailed) Vole, with its grey or russet-coloured fur, and ears so small you can hardly distinguish them. Voles too are at risk from many predators, including some snakes, and certainly from the bird that has always been associated with churchyards, the Barn Owl.

In a glass case on a bookshelf at the foot of my bed stands a stuffed Barn Owl, whose black eyes stare at me from a round white face each morning when I wake. Barn Owls on the wing often appear to be all-white, especially if you see them at dusk; but though the under-feathering is pale, the upper-feathering is a lovely golden-buff, speckled with elegant blue-grey markings and little white dots. My owl stands typically knock-kneed on its long legs, its head seemingly too big for its body.

Sadly, the number of Barn Owls has decreased to a dangerously low level, mainly due to the use of pesticides. A number of dedicated people are doing their best to help by breeding as many as possible in captivity, to be released when old enough into the care of farmers and landowners who will provide

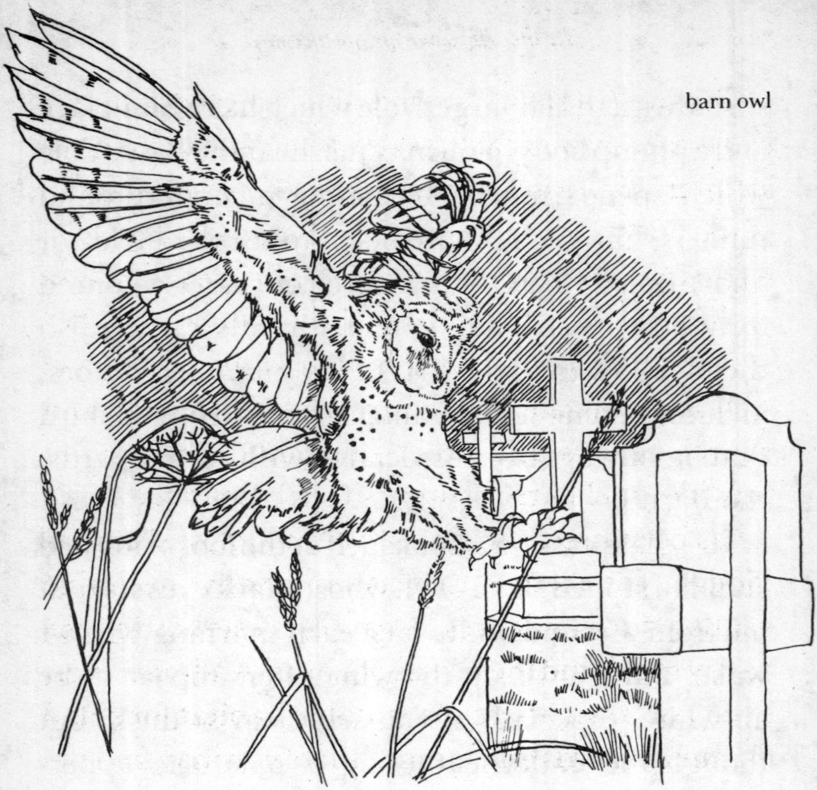

barn owl

suitable nest-sites for them in the kind of buildings they like. But still you stand less chance of seeing a Barn Owl or hearing its harsh shriek in a town churchyard than was once the case. However, Tawny Owls, the commonest of our native owls, have often been recorded right in the middle of towns, and the graveyard or cemetery is a favourite hunting-place. Unlike the Little Owl who is often about in daytime, the Tawny is nocturnal, and you may well hear it even if you don't see it.

Certainly it says 'Tu-whit!' but the most familiar call is a deep musical 'Hoo-hoo-hoo!' followed after an interval by a long tremulous 'Oo-oo-oo-oo!'. The Little Owl takes some small birds and mammals as well as worms, frogs and reptiles, but it feeds mainly on insects.

A daytime churchyard hunter is the kestrel. As well as nesting in trees, kestrels use cliff ledges, and church towers and other tall buildings in cities provide excellent substitute sites. In London, where it has been breeding since 1931, it almost seems as though the kestrel selects especially desirable gentlemen's residences, because it nests both on the Savoy Hotel and the House of Lords. And wherever, in city or town, there is a suitable habitat for small mammals, birds and insects, there you may find the kestrel hovering, ready to pounce, whether in the churchyard or in another important piece of 'country' within the town, the park.

Unlike churchyards or waste ground or rubbish dumps or railway embankments, parks are filled with people and their dogs, and so you're not all that likely to see the shyer creatures in them. Parks are generally places for the cheekier animals, like the grey squirrel and the collared dove (and of course those two commonest of townees with whom we started, the sparrow and the feral

kestrel

collared dove

pigeon). The collared dove is a comparative newcomer from Europe, first breeding in a town in Norfolk in 1955, and then spreading quickly to much of Britain. Like the pigeon, it has been quick to learn the advantages of staying close to that wasteful animal, man, and the town park suits it admirably.

I think it is a charming little bird, very elegantly designed, with pinkish-grey plumage and a distinctive, white-fringed black band that almost encircles its neck and gives it its name. In flight it has a strange wailing call, but its usual voice is a monotonous 'Coo-coo-coo' with the accent on the second coo. There's a pair that nest in a cypress tree just outside my bedroom window, and in spring and summer they start coo-*coo*-cooing as soon as it's light, and keep on and on and on like machines.

For the grey squirrel, a park must be sheer heaven. Masses of trees provide refuge and nest-sites and food in the shape of buds and shoots and bark and seeds (and eggs and baby birds); and masses of humans sit on benches and drop food everywhere in their slovenly way.

Like the collared dove the grey squirrel is an immigrant, this time from America, as its Latin name, *Sciurus carolinensis* (Carolina squirrel), tells you. A few individuals, perhaps a couple of dozen, were imported into this country at the end of the last century and now there are millions.

Like the rat (and some people – particularly foresters – call them 'tree-rats') the grey squirrel is a highly successful species, not least because, like the rat, it's quick-witted. Raiding badly designed bird-tables is squirrels' play to them, and there have been reports of squirrels hauling up bird-baskets hanging from trees hand over hand, to get at the nuts.

The grey squirrel may look cute as you watch it climbing, legs spread wide, or descending a tree head first (don't try this technique yourself), or sitting up begging for food, but in fact it's a

grey squirrel

straightforward pest, and what's more, unlike the short-lived rat, has an average life-span of twelve years. Apart from the damage it does to the bird population, taking eggs and killing babies, the root and branch of the trouble is the havoc it wreaks among trees, especially young ones. It would be unfair to blame the grey squirrel for getting its food from trees, but unfortunately it seems a naturally destructive beast, tearing off much more fruit, ripe or unripe, than is eaten, and, in particular, eating bark.

The bark of any tree carries up all the nutrients that are needed for its survival, and once the squirrel has 'ringed' a young sapling – chewed a collar of bark off, right round the trunk – the tree's a goner. The Americans knew this all right, for a couple of hundred years ago grey squirrels over there were an infinitely greater pest than they've ever been here (yet). They existed in myriads, making great migrations across the land in huge hordes that swam the rivers or lakes in their path and laid waste every field of corn they came across. Settlers in Pennsylvania killed 640,000 in 1749, and in 1808, in the State of Ohio, every man had to hand in a hundred squirrel scalps each year or pay a fine.

City parks usually contain a number of fine mature trees, and in these you may see some birds that might not visit your garden. If you hear a drumming noise, watch out for a Great Spotted Woodpecker, and you might also see a Green Woodpecker on the ground, looking for ants' nests; it's especially fond of ants, which it licks up on the

end of its very long tongue. If you're especially lucky, you could see a Lesser Spotted Woodpecker, a tiny bird not much bigger than a sparrow, but it's not easy to discern it as it creeps up the trunk of a tree.

One fascinating little park bird that climbs

nuthatch

tree-trunks is the Nuthatch. Unlike the woodpeckers, who all use their tails, flattened against the trunk, as a third leg for balancing, the Nuthatch walks up trees (or down with equal ease), clinging on with feet alone. Its sharp narrow bill is just the job for sticking into the cracks between pieces of bark to pull out the insects that lurk there, and it also has another clever trick. It sticks nuts tightly into a convenient crevice, as one would fix an object in a vice, and then hammers the nuts to split them like a man splitting logs with an axe. Hence its beak gives it its name – nut hatchet – Nuthatch.

heron

Some parks have ponds or lakes in them, and here you will see various species of waterfowl, swans, geese and ducks. I don't count these as 'wild' animals in town, but there is one urban breeding colony of a bird that can't be described as 'tame'. That bird is the Grey Heron, and the colony, which a few birds started in 1968, is in Regent's Park.

Once the birds have selected a site for a heronry, they'll go on using it year after year, building their clumsy nests high in trees, and very dirty and smelly it can get. The nests are simply rough platforms of sticks. The male collects them and the female arranges them. Herons are great fishermen, and they travel as much as a dozen miles in search of food. So if you have a pond full of goldfish in your garden and live anywhere near Regent's Park, watch out.

Watch out for all the many other birds that you are as likely to see in the park as in your own garden – blackbirds, thrushes, tits, finches, wagtails, wrens, robins – the list is endless. And there are no prizes for guessing the two creatures that dominate the scene in any park in any town. They're the birds that I began with, the pigeons and the sparrows.

Chapter 9

'PHIL-IP'

Maybe the park is a good place to end this look at some of the many animals that manage successfully to share the life of city and town with that most successful (and often least observant) of all animals, man.

Sit down for a moment on that bench in that park in the middle of that town of yours.

Use your ears to hear, not the roar of the traffic in the busy streets but a voice coming from the ground beside you. 'Phil-ip,' it says, 'Phil-ip.'

Then use your eyes, not to see the people and the houses and the shops and the office blocks, but to have a good look at the small brown bird that hops around your feet, its legs tied together by that invisible thread.

It's only a sparrow, you say?

But it's well worth watching.

BIBLIOGRAPHY

The Urban Dweller's Wildlife Companion, by Ron Wilson (Blandford Press, 1983)

The New Bird Table Book, by Tony Soper (Pan Books, 1975)

RSPB Book of Garden Birds, by Linda Bennett (Hamlyn, 1978)

Urban Foxes, by S. Harris (Whittet Books, 1986)

Spotter's Guide to Town and City Wildlife (Usborne Publications, 1981)

Man and Birds, by R. K. Murton (Collins, 1971)

A Field Guide to Birds of Britain and Europe, by Peterson, Mountford & Hollom (Collins, 1954)

A Beast Book for the Pocket, by E. Sandars (Oxford University Press, 1937)

Butterflies, by J. Moncha (Octopus Books, 1974)

Everyday Birds, by Tony Soper (David & Charles, 1976)

Badgers, by Ernest Neal (Blandford Press, 1977)

Garden and Field Birds, by J. Felix (Octopus Books, 1974)

The Observer's Book of Birds, by S. V. Benson (Frederick Warne, undated)

The Observer's Book of Wild Animals, by W. J. Stokoe (Frederick Warne, undated)

The World of Ants, Bees and Wasps, by Brian Vesey-Fitzgerald (Pelham Books, 1969)

The Sunday Times Countryside Companion, by Geoffrey Young (Country Life Books, 1985)

INDEX

Also in Puffin by Dick King-Smith

COUNTRY WATCH

Animal-watching can be fascinating and fun, if you know what to look out for and how best to observe it. As well as telling you what to look out for, *Country Watch* is full of surprising facts about animals (did you know that the tiny mole can burrow its way through thirty pounds of earth in an hour?) and Dick King-Smith has lots of marvellous stories to tell about his own encounters with animals over the years.

WATER WATCH

If you look at a map of the world, you'll see that most of its surface is sea. We are surrounded by water – all around us there are lakes, ponds, rivers and streams – not to mention man-made waterways like canals. On holiday at the seaside you can enjoy identifying all the different kinds of gull, or if you're near a rocky coastline you might even see a seal! And there are all sorts of water birds – some with very unusual habits – living near lakes and marshes.

You'd have to be lucky to spot an otter but if you're patient and observant, there are some fascinating animals to be spotted in and around a garden or village pond.

PETS FOR KEEPS

Keeping a pet can be fascinating and great fun. You don't have to be an expert either. But it *is* important to choose the right pet: one that will fit in with your family and surroundings, one that you can afford to keep, one that you will enjoy looking after, and – most important of all – one that will be happy with you. This book is packed with useful information about budgies, hamsters, cats, guinea-pigs, mice, rabbits, gerbils, canaries, bantams, rats, goldfish and dogs – any one of which might be the ideal pet for you!

Some Animal Stories from Puffin

SOUNDER

William H. Armstrong

Sounder wasn't much to look at, half bulldog, half hound, but his voice was a glory, and so was his faithfulness. But these could not help his young owner against the cruelty and indifference of the men who take away his father's liberty. A tragic and compelling tale of fortitude and courage.

THE MOUSE AND HIS CHILD

Russell Hoban

The epic journey of the father mouse and his child from the toyshop to their eventual home.

A DOG CALLED NELSON

Bill Naughton

A real life story about a one-eyed mongrel of remarkable character called Nelson. A lively, humorous and touching tale.

MRS FRISBY AND THE RATS OF NIMH

Robert C. O'Brien

A fabulous adventure about the mysterious, ultra-intelligent rats, their past and their secret connection with Mrs Frisby's late husband.

CHARLOTTE'S WEB

E. B. White

The tale of how a little girl called Fern, with the help of a friendly spider, manages to save her beloved pig Wilbur from the usual fate of nice fat little pigs.

TARKA THE OTTER

Henry Williamson

The classic tale of an otter's life and death in Devon is as true as a man's account of a wild animal can possibly be. This book was hailed as a masterpiece when first published and today Tarka is one of the best-loved creatures in world literature.

WATERSHIP DOWN

Richard Adams

One dim, moonlit night a small band of rabbits leave the comfort and safety of their warren, and set out on a long and dangerous journey. A dramatic and totally gripping bestseller.

GREYFRIARS BOBBY

Eleanor Atkinson

A touching, true story about the little Skye terrier who returned every night for fourteen years to the shepherd's grave in Greyfriars churchyard – so dearly had he loved his master.

LASSIE COME-HOME

Eric Knight

The classic heartwarming story of a dog and her devotion, who travels hundreds of miles so that she can meet a boy by the school-house gate and be faithful to her duty.

THE OTTERS' TALE

Gavin Maxwell

The enchanting true story of Gavin Maxwell's life with the three otters he kept as pets and the enormous changes they brought to his life.